THE MORAL CRISIS IN MANAGEMENT

McGRAW-HILL SERIES IN MANAGEMENT

Keith Davis, Consulting Editor

McGRAW-HILL Book Company

New York   St. Louis   San Francisco
Toronto   London   Sydney

THOMAS A. PETIT

Professor of Management
University of Arizona

the Moral Crisis in Management

THE MORAL CRISIS IN MANAGEMENT

Library of Congress Catalog Card Number 67-21597

1234567890 MR 7432106987

Preface

Alfred North Whitehead once said that a great society is one whose businessmen think greatly of their function. If this is so, America surely is a great society. Probably at no other time in the long history of business has there been as much soul-searching in the ranks of businessmen as today. Managers of big-business corporations are particularly concerned about their social function. They want to understand the meaning and legitimacy of what they do. Much of their concern can rightly be analyzed in moral terms. They want to feel that they are justified in wielding the enormous power at their disposal. They want to feel that what they do is *right*.

A quiet revolution is under way in business ethics today. The ideas, beliefs, and attitudes associated with the profit ethic are being challenged as never before. The challenge comes from the new practices professional managers are developing rather than from an ideology or doctrine. The modern manager faces a much different task than the entrepreneur of earlier generations. He has greater power than they dreamed of, but a precondition for his continued possession of this power is that it be exercised responsibly. The old idea of the divine right of capital no longer applies. Managers are forging a new ethic of social responsibility to serve as a moral guideline in day-to-day decision making, whether they realize it or not.

A major objective of this study is to put some substance into the meaningful but vague idea of social responsibility of management. Economists tend to regard this concept as either meaningless or pernicious. My view is that it is neither. Social responsibility already plays an important role in American economic life, and its importance is bound to increase in the future. Therefore, this concept is as worthy of rigorous scientific analysis as competition. To this end I have endeavored to analyze social responsibility from a positive rather than from a normative point of view.

This study is future-oriented. Its underlying hypothesis is that there is now a moral crisis in management. The profit ethic does not fit into the modern economic milieu, but it will be retained in our ideology until the ideological and theoretical foundation for the social responsibility ethic is well established. A certain looseness of style seems inevitable when an emergent process of contemporary history such as this is analyzed. So many strands of value, knowledge, fact, and social process must be interwoven that one despairs of organizing them into a coherent and rigorous analysis. Nonetheless, I felt the effort had to be made; the alternative was to drop the project entirely. Since the issue is so critical in our evolving business system, this would be too great a price to pay for stylistic niceties.

Acknowledgment is hereby given to those who helped make this book possible: William Voris, dean of the College of Business and Public Administration of the University of Arizona, who has encouraged faculty research and provided the necessary wherewithal; Harold Hoflich and David Shirley, former and present director of the Division of Economic and Business Research under whose auspices the study was carried out; the cheerful and efficient secretaries of the division who typed and retyped the manuscript; and my colleagues and students who have generously allowed me to talk of socially responsible management *ad nauseam*.

THOMAS A. PETIT

Contents

Contents

THE MORAL CRISIS IN MANAGEMENT

1

Introduction

The American economy has been through five revolutions in the twentieth century which have transformed its basic structure and method of functioning. First, the organizational revolution led to an increase in the number, size, and power of organizations of all types. Second (and an aspect of the organizational revolution), the corporate revolution expanded the scale of business enterprise and led to the dominance of the modern big-business corporation. Third, the managerial revolution saw the emergence of a class of professional managers who took over the active control of large corporations. Fourth, the property revolution separated ownership and management and diffused property rights within the corporation. Finally, the capitalist revolution brought about a change in the moral order of capitalism and greatly enlarged the public role of business and the economic role of government.[1]

These economic revolutions have altered the basic nature of the American economy to such a degree that many of the older theories about the corporation and the manager are now obsolete. Companies are supposed to have no function other than to produce goods and services, but modern corporations aid in financing education, help make foreign policy through their international operations, provide managers and workers with social status, and perform many other social functions. Businessmen are supposed to be interested only in making the largest possible profit, but most big-business managers have a strong sense of public responsibility and many of them use their power and influence to pursue broad social goals. Economic activity is supposed to be controlled by competitive forces in the market, but political influences frequently are more important.

In this changed social and economic environment, the focus of business ethics is not upon the honesty and personal foibles of businessmen so much as it is upon the relationships between the corporation, management, and society. The corporation is an autonomous institution in the sense that it is not government-run, but in carrying on its everyday affairs it is expected to further human values and serve the national purpose. Which functions it should perform in achieving these ends and how they ought to be performed, rather than matters of ordinary honesty and fastidiousness, are at the core of business ethics today.[2]

Ethics presents a problem for many managers today. They are concerned about the ethical consequences of their actions because they are uncertain which ends the enterprise should pursue and which means should be used to attain these ends. If managers had no discretion in these matters, there would be no ethical problem. But since they do control the destinies of the corporations which they manage, it matters very much which alternative courses of action they decide to carry out. Managers realize that because of the enormous economic and social power which they possess they cannot help but play a key role in determining the directions taken by the rapidly changing American society. They want to use their power wisely and in the best interests of all concerned, but they are not sure how to do this.

The Profit Ethic

The profit ethic is the traditional ethical standard of business conduct in capitalistic systems. According to it the businessman makes decisions *solely on the basis of which alternative will contribute the most to profits.*[3] The only values he considers are those which can be expressed in monetary terms. To many, the logic of this ethic seems heartless, cruel, selfish, and even dishonest. Under the profit-maximization rule, a man might fire an old and faithful employee and hire an unknown off the street who offers to work at a lower wage. Or he might fool buyers by promoting shoddy merchandise at quality prices.

Although some businessmen use the profit ethic to rationalize base and underhanded business practices, most do not. The majority believe in it because it was founded on a well-developed philosophy embracing some of the noblest values in Western civilization. The theory of how the economy works, developed by the eighteenth- and nineteenth-century British school of classical economics, provides the philosophical foundation for the profit ethic. There are four basic assumptions underlying this theory:

1 *Natural law:* There are natural laws governing the social activities of men just as there are physical laws governing nature.
2 *Universal competition:* Competition among individuals in free markets is the natural law of economic life.
3 *"Economic man":* Men are rational and entirely motivated to further their own economic self-interest.

4 *Harmony of interests:* Natural economic laws impose a social harmony that eliminates conflict among individuals and between the individual and society.

A body of thought developed, based on these assumptions, which gave the businessman an ethical basis for pursuing his economic self-interest. He was convinced that, at the same time, he was acting in the best interests of society. The businessman looked upon himself as a small cog in the divine order of things. He was simply doing the "natural thing" by maximizing profits. If everyone in the economy—producers, customers, resource owners, and workers—did the same thing, it would produce the best possible social economic result. By narrowly focusing on profits, the businessman actually made his best possible contribution to society because that was the way the system worked. It was the economic system which the businessman believed best upheld the cardinal values of freedom, democracy, progress, and justice.

The profit ethic arose in eighteenth-century Great Britain, but it reached its zenith of acceptance by both business and the public in America during the period between the Civil War and World War I. This era—known as the Age of Enterprise—was one of accelerated economic development. The great drive in American society was aimed at industrialization. Everyone was in favor of progress, and progress in the rural and agrarian society of that period was closely tied to the goal of rapid industrialization. Such a powerful social goal was bound to have a strong impact on business ethics.

To attain the goal of rapid industrialization vast quantities of tools, machines, factories, and equipment had to be accumulated in a fairly short time. In view of the relatively weak national government and the prevailing policy of *laissez faire,* this could only be accomplished by businessmen earning huge profits and plowing them back into industry. Thus entrepreneurs were motivated to create whole new industries in pursuit of profit. They were allowed by society to pursue their largely self-seeking ends because they paralleled those of the nation. It was a good bargain on both sides. The businessmen earned enormous profits and became wealthy; society got the capital it needed for an industrial economy and a higher standard of living.

Most Americans accepted the idea that businessmen were making a great contribution to social welfare by maximizing profits and reinvesting them since they generally distrusted central government and advocated intense individualism. The limited-liability law that recognized the corporation as a legal person was commonly interpreted to be a device allowing businessmen to pursue self-interest without being held personally responsible. The Darwinian theory of the struggle for existence and survival of the fittest was influential in social thought, and it too supported the profit ethic.

The profit ethic served businessmen well in the Age of Enterprise. They accomplished their ends with a full-bodied gusto that is disappearing in the modern business world. Rights of private property were so strongly entrenched that little attention was given to questions of the social responsibility of business and the legitimacy of management power. The businessman's religious beliefs helped harmonize his philosophy and ethical ideas. The Ten Commandments were widely considered as firm and sophisticated an ethical foundation as a businessman needed. The first four commandments reminded him of his personal relationship to God, and the last six admonished him not to do such things as kill, steal, or lie in pursuit of private gain.

The five economic revolutions in the twentieth century have transformed the structure and functioning of the American economy and undermined the profit ethic. Most economists now consider the assumptions underlying the classical theory of economics to have been originally oversimplifications at best. The gap between the assumptions and social and economic reality has widened steadily in the twentieth century, however, so that what at first were merely oversimplifications are now invalid and misleading generalizations. Findings in sociology, anthropology, and social psychology have made it difficult to believe that immutable natural laws control man's social relations and his destiny. The decline of price competition in capitalist countries and the rise of other noncompetitive economic systems have challenged the assumption of universal competition. Increasing knowledge of the complexities of human motivation has destroyed the economic-man concept. The assumption of harmony of interests has lost ground in democratic societies where there is a desire to bring conflicts between individuals and groups into the open in order to resolve them peacefully.

It is no longer widely believed that if individuals use their powers, resources, and energies to pursue self-interest the best overall social result inevitably will be produced. We recognize that there are conflicts between private and public goals. In conducting his professional affairs the businessman, like the senator, general, and bishop, is expected to consider the public interest ahead of his private interest if they are not the same. Few people still believe that the businessman *necessarily* furthers social economic welfare by making as much money as possible.

Economists who have studied management behavior in recent years reject the idea that managers have no goal other than profit maximization. Among other goals, they have found the desires to remain financially liquid, to maintain a share of the market, to grow and expand, to be conservative in financing, to attain a high level of efficiency, and to protect existing profit levels. Although these goals could conceivably contribute to long-run profits, a second type of personal "nonprofit" goal of managers does not. Not consistent with the profit ethic are the desires of managers to substitute leisure for work, to be their own bosses, to be free from worry, to retain control of the enterprise, and to consider matters of public welfare in administering the enterprise.

Some economists conclude that there are technical obstacles to prevent managers from maximizing profit (e.g., problems of computing costs), but that even if this were not the case, they would not maximize profits because of moral scruples.[4] Most managers today would probably agree.[5] They do not have the demand and supply data required to rationally determine price and output levels which maximize profits. Furthermore, there is a diffusion of decision making in modern business not taken into account in economic theory.

A balanced view is that profit is an important goal of business but managers need not maximize profits. Profit is necessary to the survival of the enterprise and is needed to attain other objectives. But most managers are content to earn a satisfactory level of profit rather than hold out for the maximum obtainable. In the press of modern business where decisions must be made rapidly and often from sketchy data, it is too difficult to determine the profit-maximizing decision or policy. Most managers "muddle through" and do the best they can. This approach is known as "profit satisficing"[6] as compared to "profit maximizing."

The Social Responsibility Ethic

Changes in the roles of the corporation and the manager have brought about changes in the motives and personalities of the men who direct

American industry. At the turn of the century the businessman looked forward to leading the rapidly industrializing society to greater heights of productivity and wealth than ever attained before. To do this he needed power. He became a "power seeker" who actively sought power and delighted in its use. Today the power seeker is being replaced by a new kind of manager, one who underplays the amount of power he possesses. The modern manager tends to be a "business moralist." He knows that he must use power to get his job done. However, he fears the consequences to the welfare of the corporation and his own personality if that power is fully exercised. It is likely that the business moralist will emerge as our next business hero.[7]

What are the causes of such a shift of management motives and personality? The very success of the businessman has created new social responsibilities for him. When the standard of living in this country was low, the first order of business was to expand the flow of goods and services that people needed and wanted. The power-seeking businessman led in transforming a rural farming society into one huge factory. Mankind's ancient foe of poverty now has been defeated for the majority of American citizens.

The modern manager has thoroughly earned his high place among the leaders of the nation. But his responsibilities have kept pace with the increase in importance of his social role. People want other things besides goods and services from the modern corporation. Increasingly, it is considered the manager's job to see that they get them.

There has been a decline in the broad public support of the power-seeking type of businessman. When the nation was first industrializing, his approach was in harmony with general ethical standards. Power is needed in any period of rapid mobilization of resources to accomplish broad social goals. But once these goals have been accomplished, there generally is a negative reaction to the concentration of power, and the public clamors for its dispersal or control by society. During wartime the government takes over virtually all power to wage the war, but at war's end there is a strong urge to disarm and "get back to normalcy." The early drive toward industrialization can be looked upon as a war to defeat the enemy of poverty. That war has been largely won. The American people are no longer willing to accept managers who openly exult in their power.

Modern professional managers are well aware of this attitude. They recognize that they must be careful in the use of the vast power they possess. They no longer defend this power as the divine right of capital. They are fearful that if they do not accept the full social responsibilities which go with the power, they will lose it, probably to someone antagonistic to business management and free enterprise. Some leading executives think that the reconstruction of the moral foundation of business is the most urgent problem facing American business today. This is why they are searching for new precepts to replace the old ones based merely on profit maximization. The ethic of socially responsible management is a result of this search.

A *New York Times* survey conducted to learn the ideas of fifty-two leading executives of the largest corporations about the social responsibilities of management is revealing. "The sampling found every executive who replied emphatic in expressing his belief that business had a social responsibility beyond providing quality goods and services to consumers."[8] The respondents thought of themselves as "environmentalists"—administrators who must integrate their enterprises into society. George S. Moore, president of the First National City Bank, New York, put it this way:

> Social responsibility is not an attitude that a business organization adopts in a fit of benevolence like a decision to hold a company picnic. Its social responsibility is, instead, inseparable from its response to the kind of world in which we live. For today's institutions—banking or business, public or private—cannot exist in modern society without reacting constructively to (1) the goals of society, and (2) the economic, technological, social and political forces that mold that society.[9]

The executives pointed out that a business enterprise must earn a profit to survive and grow, but none of them took the position that a firm should maximize profits. They believed that management cannot escape responsibility for balancing the interests of stockholders with those of other groups in society. As Lammot du Pont Copeland, president of Du Pont, said, "Management, it seems to me, must reach for a balanced solution within the framework of one unassailable precept: business is a means to an end for society and not an end in itself, and therefore business must act in concert with a broad public interest and serve objectives of mankind and society or it will not survive."[10]

Some evidences of socially responsible management are the participation by executives in political affairs, corporate support of educational institutions, various employee welfare measures, community relations programs, and intensified public relations campaigns. These activities are considered essential to safeguard the position of the corporation, and sometimes they are justified on this basis alone. "A prudent regard for all the interests that merge in making the business a going concern now and in the future is, in fact, the only way to protect and to augment shareholder equity."[11]

Social responsibility of management is not, however, merely a public relations gesture that has as its objective the protection of the firm's profit position. "Self-conscious dedication to social responsibility may have started as a purely defensive maneuver against strident attacks on big corporations and on the moral efficacy of the profit system. But defense alone no longer explains the motive."[12] There is a sincere desire on the part of responsible executives to gain the respect of the general public by utilizing their considerable power for the common good. The corporation is regarded as a multipurpose social institution, and the pursuit of profit is secondary in importance to the public interest.

The Trend toward Social Responsibility

The viewpoint and functions of the managers of large corporations exemplify the age of big business. Many top managers have been trained professionally in graduate schools of business administration. There are other new types of executives who have come into administrative positions with backgrounds in the sciences or engineering. Whatever their training and background, modern managers have a professional attitude toward their work. They recognize that only those executives who get results are considered successful. A manager must guide his company so it can survive, make profits, and grow in an ever-changing America; otherwise he is a failure. A manager whose company continually has antagonistic relations with customers, labor, or government is not doing a good job.

The modern manager is expected to produce results in accordance with a practical as well as a professional code developed in the business world. An important aspect of this code is the manager's strong sense of responsibility to the public. At one time management was well regarded if it satisfied the owners and customers. Later company employees and their unions also had to be considered. Now some big-business corporations, those in steel, for example, must justify price increases before congressional committees—unthinkable a generation ago. Because the modern big-business corporation is responsible to many different groups and interests, the manager is more like a public official than an entrepreneur. The modern manager could not function effectively if he had the "public be damned" attitude of some of the nineteenth-century captains of industry. A more appropriate attitude is "the public be cultivated."[13]

One reason for the basic change in management attitudes and motivations is the increasing depersonalization resulting from corporate growth. Highly professional skills are required to run huge industrial corporations. Accounting, labor relations, product research, and a host of other specialized modern business functions are carried on by departments in the corporation. The position of a department head is an office defined in terms of specific skills and functions with no reference to the individual filling the office. Today we have the kind of bureaucratization of private enterprise that Max Weber foresaw when he predicted it would be the destiny of industrial man to live in an "iron cage of bureaucracy."

There is a big difference between the values and motivations of the nineteenth-century entrepreneur and the twentieth-century management bureaucrat. The entrepreneur was intent on winning his fortune; today's management bureaucrat seeks to discharge the duties of his office.

The attitude of modern managers toward profit is markedly different from that of the entrepreneur of yesteryear. The separation of ownership and control in the large corporation has given managers a good deal of autonomy. They have been freed from the necessity of pursuing profit single-mindedly in the stockholder's interest. Now they can emphasize other objectives such as their own prestige; the leadership of the company in the industry; and the welfare of employees, customers, and community. Goals associated with the ethic of social responsibility have come to occupy almost as important a place as profit in the objectives of some corporations. Many top managers behave as if they believe that they and their companies are responsible for many of the social and political problems of modern industrial society. Of course not all top managers accept or even comprehend the idea that broad public accountability is part of the modern responsibility of business, but the trend is definitely in this direction.

Most managers still cling in thought to the profit ethic despite the trend toward social responsibility in their behavior. The legitimacy of profit is a central article of the American business creed.[14] The free enterprise system is a profit system, it is argued, and to question profits is to attack the system. The creed defends profit on the ground that profit recipients deserve what they get because they perform a valuable service to society. Profit, it is claimed, fulfills a necessary social function which otherwise would not be performed so well or so cheaply. The primary justification of profit is that it is earned by giving customers what they want in freely competitive markets. Underlying this view of profit is the assumption that the firm performs only an economic function and that the job of management is to see that this function is performed efficiently. Profit is thus an objective measurement of the firm's efficiency in allocating resources. Managers see themselves as decision makers who are highly rational, realistic, practical, and "hard-boiled." They resist any suggestion that the firm performs noneconomic functions which call for decisions that cannot be made on the basis of the profit ethic.

Thus there is a gap between business practice and business ethics. Most managers claim to accept the profit ethic and to reject the social responsibility ethic. Yet their behavior departs significantly from profit maximization in the direction of social responsibility. The gap between business practice and the ethical beliefs of managers is the cause of the moral crisis of management.

Resolution of the Moral Crisis in Management

A business ethic, to be acceptable to society, must be compatible with prevailing economic ideology and theory. An ideology is a system of beliefs intended to influence action or opinion. "It is a system of thought through which runs some central theme, such as women, government, God, mankind, the white race, the family, or property."[15] The ideologies of a society organize prevailing views of the world into a "logical" system. There is an intimate relation between ideology and business ethics. A business ethic must be consistent with the moral code of society, and the ideologies shared by the members of society are the source of this moral code. Science is itself a kind of ideology since it is ultimately based on a system of beliefs which help man to organize his views of the world into a logical system. Indeed, science is one of modern industrial society's most powerful ideologies. Therefore, any business ethic which is accepted by the general public and the business community must be fitted into the society's system of ideology and the picture of the business and economic world provided by the science of economics.

The end of *laissez faire* and the rise of the general-welfare state have undermined the profit ethic by contradicting the basic assumption that the best individual and social result ensues when individuals pursue their self-interest in untrammeled freedom. The new dispensation emphasizes cooperation rather than competition, social interdependence rather than rugged individualism, and the human rather than supernatural source of social and economic arrangements. The hard-driving profit maximizer who eschews all values not definable in money terms is out of step with such a welfare-oriented ideology.

The classical economics has also fallen in stature during the twentieth century. The rise of big business has wrecked havoc upon the nicely worked out deductions of Adam Smith and the other classical economists by invalidating the assumptions upon which they were based. The key element in their analysis—the competitive market made up of many small buyers and sellers who freely interact—has disappeared in most industries. The large corporation has brought about oligopolistic markets in which price competition gives way to advertising, sales promotion, product differentiation, and artificial obsolescence. It has also brought about the separation of ownership and control and the development of a professional management elite with functions, values, operating methods, and motives quite different from those of the nineteenth-century entrepreneur. Today few academic economists defend the unalloyed profit motive except as a useful fiction, and a group of younger economists is actively developing the new field of managerial capitalism to bring theory more into line with reality.

It is because of the uncertain state of contemporary economic ideology and economic theory that there is a moral crisis in management. The pace of change in the economy and society in recent years has been so rapid that there has not been time for the development of a new ideology to replace *laissez faire* or a new economic theory to replace the classical economics. This is understandable, given the nature of ideology and science. All ideologies are inherently conservative. Men do not like to give up ideas to which they have grown accustomed about the nature of their world. They will do so only if it is clear that a once satisfactory ideology has become a "sacred cow" which no longer is in touch with reality and has lost its purpose. Economics, like other social sciences, follows a very uneven course, backtracking and going off on fruitless tangents at times. There is a natural reluctance on the part of economists to give up parts of the body of received economic theory which have the sanctification of long usage. But once it becomes clear that changes in the empirical world which are inconsistent with economic theory are permanent, forces inevitably are brought to bear to change the erroneous assumptions and deductions.

We are at a turning point in business ethics because the inadequacy of the profit ethic is becoming clearly recognized, and an ideological and scientific foundation is being laid for the ethic of social responsibility. At first only a few free-thinking executives dared take issue with the prevailing business ideology. Today ethical soul-searching is becoming a conventional practice among top managers. They seek a philosophy to aid them in understanding who they are and what they should do. Social scientists, management consultants, business statesmen, and other intellectuals concerned with modern business and its problems are busy forging the concepts, ideas, theories, and other ideological and scientific elements needed to support the ethic of social responsibility which already is practiced widely. Economists are revising the theory of the firm; sociologists are becoming interested in the broad relations between the corporate organization and society; thoughtful executives are placing their ideas before the business community; and management consultants are focusing attention upon the nebulous and philosophical problems of how to guide corporations through the choppy seas of social change.

In the long run it is inevitable that business ethics will become congruent with existing management practice. Men cannot long accept a status quo that is not rationalized by generally accepted ideology and theory. But before the gap between management practice and ethical beliefs is bridged many individuals must contribute to the emergent process of resolution of the moral crisis in management. The purpose of this book is to point out the true nature of this crisis. It has been produced by ground swells of social change that are unavoidable in a highly dynamic industrial society like ours with a cultural heritage of freedom and mobility. It is important that the true nature of the crisis is understood so that appropriate steps may be taken to resolve it. It would be disastrous, for example, if the remedy sought were more government controls over business. In the long run a deeper understanding of the relations between the manager, corporation, and society is the most effective means to a satisfactory resolution of the moral crisis of management.

NOTES

1 Each of these revolutions will be analyzed in detail in Chapter 2.

2 Peter Drucker, "Big Business and the National Purpose," *Harvard Business Review,* vol. 40, no. 2 (March–April, 1962), pp. 49–59.

3 A distinction should be made at this point between the "profit motive" and the "profit ethic." The profit motive means nothing more than that businessmen are motivated to earn profit. It can coexist with other motives (e.g., employee welfare, community development). The profit ethic, on the other hand, implies that the only motive of the businessman is profit maximization. It does not allow other motives to coexist.

4 Robert N. Anthony, "The Trouble with Profit Maximization," *Harvard Business Review,* vol. 38, no. 6 (November–December, 1960), pp. 126–134.

5 Father Raymond C. Baumhart, S.J., found in a survey of businessmen that 94 percent of the respondents believed that spiritual, ethical, moral, and social considerations should, and do, influence their business behavior. See his article "How Ethical Are Businessmen?" *Harvard Business Review,* vol. 39, no. 4 (July–August, 1961), pp. 7–19, 156–176.

6 Herbert A. Simon, *Models of Man* (New York: John Wiley & Sons, Inc., 1957), pp. 204–205.

7 Eugene E. Jennings, "Make Way for the Business Moralist," *Nation's Business,* vol. 47, no. 9 (September, 1959), pp. 90–96.

8 Robert A. Wright, "Beyond the Profits: Business Reaches for a Social Role," *The New York Times* (July 3, 1966), p. 1F.

9 *Ibid.*

10 *Ibid.,* p. 16F.

11 Richard Eells, "Social Responsibility: Can Business Survive the Challenge?" *Business Horizons,* vol. 2, no. 4 (Winter, 1959), p. 41.

12 Theodore Levitt, "The Dangers of Social Responsibility," *Harvard Business Review,* vol. 36, no. 5 (September–October, 1959), p. 41.

13 Wilbert E. Moore, *The Conduct of the Corporation* (New York: Random House, Inc., 1962), chap. XXI.

14 Francis X. Sutton, Seymour E. Harris, Carl Kaysen, and James Tobin, *The American Business Creed* (Cambridge, Mass.: Harvard University Press, 1956).

15 Richard T. LaPiere, *Sociology* (New York: McGraw-Hill Book Company, 1946), p. 285.

2

The Five Revolutions

Now let us look at the changes in technology and organization which have caused the gap between business practice and ethics. The American economy has been transformed in the twentieth century by the organizational, corporate, managerial, property, and capitalist revolutions. This chapter describes these revolutions and analyzes their impact on business ethics.

The Organizational Revolution

The rise of bureaucracy reflects the growing importance of large organizations in virtually every area of social life. Boulding called our attention to this movement in his book *The Organizational Revolution*. He pointed out that there has been a worldwide increase in the number, size, and power of organizations, especially those whose activity is directed toward the economic betterment of their members. He felt this movement to be of such consequence that it deserved the name "the organizational revolution." Evidences of this revolution are found in the expansion in scale of corporations, labor unions, farm organizations, professional associations, and government.[1]

The organizational revolution is a product of the earlier Industrial Revolution. The great increase in productivity brought about by improved technology has enabled the industrial age to sustain a much larger population than ever before. It is an increasingly urban population: The number of people living in cities of one hundred thousand or more increased from 16 million at the beginning of the twentieth century to 314 million by mid-century. The changes in technology and population have led to the development of a new industrial way of life. In preindustrial times the majority of mankind lived in folk society—small, close knit, self-sufficient, and rural human groups. Modern industrial man lives in mass society. He is increasingly dependent upon large and complex organizations for the attainment of social, political, and economic goals.

The desire of men to improve their economic lot by more efficient economic organizations is a major cause of the organizational revolution. People in nearly every nation in the world strongly desire to achieve a higher standard of living. The most rapid way to attain this goal today is to industrialize, and this involves a greater organizational effort than in preindustrial society. Modern machine technology is based on the rationalization of effort and planning and requires a high level of organization for maximum effectiveness. A second cause of the organizational revolution is our greater capacity to construct and operate large-scale organizations. Technological changes in communication and transportation have made it possible to coordinate much larger aggregations of men and machines. Professional organizers and administrators have learned how to push back the point at which organizations run into diseconomies of scale and become inefficient.

Examples of bureaucratic organizations are corporations, unions, government agencies, churches, pressure groups, trade associations, universities, and hospitals. Despite their different functions, these organizations have the same basic bureaucratic characteristics. The leaders of each one strive to be rational in the conscious adaption of means to ends. Each has an operating charter: "a conscious and deliberate attempt to adapt the structure and personnel of the organization to the most efficient achievement of goals prescribed by the top leaders in, or outside, the bureaucracy."[2]

The pyramid-shaped organizational structure of bureaucracies enables a relatively small number of people at the top to control a large number of people below. The range of decisions each member of a bureaucracy can make is clearly defined and limited. This leads to a high degree of specialization of skill and function within the organization.

Three technical gains in organizational effectiveness are made possible by bureaucratic structure. First, a few leaders can coordinate the actions of relatively large numbers of people. In small organizations the members are able to maintain direct face-to-face contact with one another. But in large organizations this is physically impossible, and the coordination required to carry out complicated tasks requires setting up the hierarchal arrangements typical of bureaucracy. A second gain of bureaucracies is greater facility for making complex decisions which are beyond the competence of any single individual. Where the number of variables or amount of information required to make decisions is extensive, bureaucracy is an aid to rational calculation. An example is the production of automobiles. Such varied engineering, design, manufacturing, sales, and advertising "know-how" is needed to produce and market automobiles that only a bureaucracy can do the job. Finally, there is the gain of division of labor. Generally, the greater the division of labor in an organization the less face-to-face contact there is between the members and the greater the need for bureaucracy.

The machine ultimately is the cause of the organizational revolution, and the society that it is creating resembles a machine. The machine is a marvel of organization. It consists of a number of parts that have no meaning or function except in the way that they relate to each other. Each part makes its special contribution to the total result of the machine. There is no extraneous part or movement—the machine is a complete rationalization of a particular field of action. This characteristic of functional interdependence of parts also has relevance for society. If industrial society is to take maximum advantage of machine technology, it must accept the logic of machine organization. The parts of society must have the same precise relationship of functional interdependence as the parts of a machine. Such a society, which can appropriately be termed an *organizational society,* is emerging in the contemporary United States.

The economy of the organizational society is a mixed economy which preserves much of the capitalist price system but uses public and private organizations to improve the economic position of lower income groups and to prevent depressions. In developing the organizational economy, we are following a path halfway between the low level of organization of laissez-faire capitalism and the all-out organizational effort of communism. We have taken this course because there no longer is a simple choice to be made between control or noncontrol by organizations of the economic processes in modern industrial society. The only real choice is between the totalitarian control of the state and a more pluralistic and democratic system of control. The difference between these two approaches is the basis of the ideological conflict between the United States and Russia.

It appears beyond dispute that the reason why we have an organizational society is because most people prefer it to other ways of organizing modern society. However, this type of social organization does pose serious problems for us. Our heritage of values and ideals is threatened by the organizational way of life. There is no doubt, for example, that individualism is difficult to sustain in giant organizations. The way to protect this and other traditional values and ideals is not to do away with organizations, however, but to see to it that we develop organizations that are compatible with the American way of life. We have long since passed the point in our national development where we have a choice between organizations and something else. Our only choice now is between organizations that serve our needs and those that do not.[3]

The Corporate Revolution

The American business corporation has undergone a profound transformation during the last half century or so. It has grown tremendously in size. In many industries the entire output is now produced by a few companies (e.g., automobiles, aluminum, cigarettes, typewriters, chemicals, tires, and chewing gum). The tremendous concentration of power in big business has led to a market structure which favors nonprice rather than price competition. It has also increased the political, social, and cultural significance of the corporation and thus altered the role that it plays in society. All of these changes collectively are referred to as the *corporate revolution.*

The importance of the very large corporation in today's economy is indicated by the Billion Dollar Club. In 1963 there were sixty members of this club, each with annual sales of at least one billion dollars. Their combined sales totaled 121.7 billion dollars, 29.5 percent of all United States manufacturing sales. They controlled 35.3 percent of the nation's manufacturing assets. Not only do these mammoth enterprises make up a substantial part of American industry, but they are the pacesetters of the business community as well. Increasingly, such giants as General Motors, General Electric, Standard Oil of New Jersey, and Du Pont lead the way in product research, labor-management relations, management practices, business ethics, and other areas of business activity. The relatively small number of big-business corporations is no indication, therefore, of their total impact on the American economy. As Drucker has pointed out, the institution which is representative rather than average, is the one which sets the standard; and this is the large corporation in contemporary American society.[4]

Managers in industries dominated by giant corporations have learned that it does not pay to compete strongly on price. They all are faced with the same problem of heavy overhead costs. When a company's sales go down there is a natural inclination to lower price in order to maintain the sales volume needed to cover fixed costs. If a seller is successful in doing this, however, he will antagonize his rivals by taking business away from them and they can be expected to retaliate. Only the customers can benefit from the price war that ensues. It is more sensible, from the standpoint of the large sellers, to avoid aggressive price competition and follow a policy of "live and let live."

In industries in which big business prevails, the price generally is set by administrative decision for a period of time, a selling season, for example, and each firm adjusts production to suit the demand for its product at the established price. Usually one firm acts as the price leader for the industry. Once the price has been set, it is not changed unless there is a marked shift in industry cost or demand conditions. When a change in price is made, it follows a definite pattern of price leadership. Thus there tends to be more price stability and uniformity in large industries than in those made up of many small firms, where the market price may change rapidly in response to short-run shifts in supply and demand.[5]

Important as the large corporation is as a producer of goods and services, it cannot be understood solely in economic terms. Its influence today far transcends the marketplace. It is more than an economic institution; it also is a political, social, and cultural entity. It is a potent political force in many communities and most states because of its vast economic power. Few nooks or crannies in the economy have escaped the influence of the large corporation. Aside from the state, it is our most dominant social institution. It sets the tone for education, religion, and other social institutions, thus touching virtually every aspect of our lives. In little more than half a century, big business has moved from the periphery to the center of our social existence.

From the standpoint of managers and workers, the giant corporation is not merely a place in which men earn their living. It is a complex environment in which they spend most of their lives, and they expect more from it than a salary or wage. They want freedom and justice from big business and a sense of personal identity in a mass society where the individual is made to feel weak and isolated at every turn. In return they are expected to pledge their loyalty to the company. This is particularly true of upper-level managers for whom complete domination by the organization's personality is probably the single most important qualification for holding office. The modern corporation aspires to the status of a social institution, on the level of the church, family, and territorial community, in its efforts to gain the allegiance of men.[6]

The large corporation also influences American society through what Max Lerner calls "the reach of the business spirit."[7] This spirit is exemplified by the principle of action upon which business is based—market sale for a profit. This principle has become applied in an increasing number of noneconomic areas of life. Erich Fromm has described the marketing

orientation toward life, which looks upon even such activities as marriage in terms of a process of exchange in which each individual attempts to maximize what he or she "can get in the market." The values and goals associated with success in big business—prestige, money, power, security—have become the most important common denominators in evaluating individual performance in all areas of American life.

Change in the role of the corporation in society is seen most clearly in the new functions it has taken on. The prime function of the corporation is still economic—to produce and distribute goods and services. But the corporation is something more than an economic entity. It is a political organization because of the great power it possesses, and it is a welfare institution because of its influence on individual and social welfare. The corporation is also a social institution because the cooperative efforts of many people with different interests are necessary to carry on its operations, and it is a cultural entity since its activities occur within a framework of commonly shared beliefs about how people should behave. In each of these areas the corporation performs *noneconomic functions:*

1 *Political functions:* generally considered to be the responsibility of government, such as the making of foreign policy by international oil companies
2 *Welfare functions:* to further individual and public welfare, such as corporate donations to help finance private colleges, and the loaning of executives for charitable and civic betterment programs in the community
3 *Social functions:* which meet a need of society, such as the provision of a social status based on occupation for workers and managers
4 *Cultural functions:* which influence the beliefs, values, and goals of the members of society; for example, the application of the criteria of success in business to nonbusiness areas of life

Thus the corporate revolution did more than merely expand the size of business enterprise; it transformed the basic character of American business. The earliest corporations were mainly legal devices to facilitate the private business transactions of individuals. The modern large corporation still serves this purpose but now it is something more: It is the prime agency for organizing our economic and social life. In a business-oriented civilization like ours in which the economic aspects of life are in the forefront, this is tantamount to saying that the corporation is the key social institution. We now have a "corporate system" which is as important in our industrial era as the feudal system was in the agrarian Middle Ages.

The Managerial Revolution

The formation of the corporate giants at the turn of the century ushered in the managerial revolution. It marked an end to one era of business management and the beginning of another. The passing of Andrew Carnegie from the scene of active business leadership when his interests were merged into United States Steel symbolized the end of the regime of the captains of industry and the dawning of the new age of the professional manager.

The most striking characteristic of the modern manager is his autonomy from owners. In theory, the stockholders elect a board of directors which looks after the interests of the owners by formulating the broad policies of the company and selecting top management personnel. In most large corporations, however, practice is exactly the opposite of theory. The management group selects its own slate of candidates to fill vacancies on the board, and the stockholders merely ratify their choices. The reason for this turnabout is the passivity of the numerous stockholders. They are mainly interested in dividends and the chance for a capital gain in the value of their stock. The average stockholder is indifferent to the board's function of overseeing management as long as the company is not obviously badly managed.

Stockholders generally do not object to management determining its own broad policies. Management men who are members of the board of directors tend to dominate them. This means that, in effect, the managers report to themselves. Since they are in the position of being able to reappoint themselves as officers of the corporation, there seems to be no outside check on their actions.

It is sometimes asserted that the stockholder has been deprived of his rights of control and decision by managers who lust for power. The opposite is true. The stockholder has actually thrust aside his rights of control and decision. The failure of efforts to develop the concept of "stockholder democracy" indicates that nothing can be done to induce him to reassume his rights. They are a burden to him because they are contrary to his purpose in becoming a stockholder (i.e., to earn a return on his investment). If he is dissatisfied with the management of the corporation, he sells his shares and invests in another company. Compared to other groups who have an interest in the corporation—managers, workers, customers, suppliers—the stockholder can sever his relationship with the corporation with remarkable ease. Therefore, it would be more correct to designate him as a "stockholder-investor" or a "stockholder-depositor," rather than a "stockholder-owner."[8]

The most important aspect of the managerial revolution in relation to this study, of course, is the weakening of the profit motive. Profit in the managerial ideology is no longer a goal to be sought for its own sake; it is now valued for its usefulness to society. Charles E. Wilson, while president of General Motors, characterized profit as "the food on which American industry has grown to an unchallenged position of leadership and usefulness in the world's economy." M. E. Coyle of General Motors emphasized the advantage of profit to others rather than the owners: "The hope of making a profit is fundamentally responsible for industrial progress. This is the incentive function of profits—an incentive to efficiency as well as to product improvement." Robert G. Dunlop of the Sun Oil Company viewed profit as a means rather than an end in itself: "Profits must be seen as a working part of the dynamic institutional structure we call our free competitive enterprise system. As such, profits perform definite and vital functions."[9]

If big-business managers do not base decisions on the profit motive, what do they base them on? The answer is that there is no single guide similar to the profit motive that managers follow in making decisions. Rather, they conceive of their function and that of the enterprise in broad enough terms to visualize several objectives, all of importance for the corporation's survival and well-being. Drucker has stated that *"no one simple objective is 'the' objective of a business; no one single yardstick 'the' measure of performance, prospects, and results of a business; no one single area 'the' most important area."*[10] Such measures as return on investment, share of the market, and so on are only indicators of a multidimensional process of survival. Drucker lists as areas that influence managerial decision making the five following "survival functions" of business enterprise:[11]

1 The enterprise needs, first, *a human organization designed for joint performance* and capable of perpetuating itself. . . .

2 The second survival objective arises from the fact that the enterprise exists in *society and economy.* . . .

3 Then, of course, there is the area of the specific purpose of business, of its contribution. The purpose is certainly to *supply an economic good and service.* . . .

4 There is another purpose characteristic which I would, so to speak, call the nature of the beast; namely, that this all happens in a *changing* economy and a *changing* technology. . . .

5 Finally, there is an absolute requirement of survival, namely that of *profitability,* for the very simple reason that everything I have said so far spells out *risk.*

The managerial revolution was inevitable, given our advanced state of industrialization. But the form it has taken has been strongly influenced by the American value system. Because of our democratic orientation, we favor informal and nonauthoritarian mechanisms of social control. We naturally looked first to the market as the basic means of social control of economic activity. But we also are strongly materialistic, and most of us believe that big business is largely responsible for our high standard of living. We have accepted big-business economic structure and the inevitable decline in competition to which its concentration of economic power has led. We have not been willing to use the antitrust weapon to break up big business and restore the competitive economic structure of an earlier day because we do now want to give up the high productivity of big business and because we are reluctant to engage in overt economic planning.

The Property Revolution

The separation of ownership and control resulting from the corporate and managerial revolutions has changed the concept of corporate property. The typical stockholder in a large corporation provides a share of the capital necessary for production, but he gives up control over how that capital is used to the management of the company. All that he has left is a claim on a share of the profits as dividends and the right to sell his interests, hopefully at a capital gain. The spiritual value of ownership—the satisfaction of creatively utilizing productive assets—is gone. All that the stockholder actually "owns" is a piece of paper that gives him certain rights to the benefits of property. It is only this that he can use or dispose of, not the assets of the issuing corporation.

The property revolution consisted of a diffusion of rights to the same concrete object. In America the traditional conception of "private property" emphasized concentration of all property rights in the hands of an individual owner. There is no reason, however, why various kinds of rights cannot attach to the same object. "Property consists, first, not of things, but of rights; it is not a concrete object of reference, but a socially recognized claim."[12] A broad distinction can be made between the right of control and the right of beneficial ownership. Berle and Means used the concepts of "active property" and "passive property" to make this distinction.[13] Active property involves control of how property is used without enjoying benefits derived from it; passive property confers the right to enjoy the benefits of property without having the right to determine how property is used.

Thus instead of asking, "Who owns the corporation?" we should ask, "What rights are represented in corporate property?" Clearly corporate property does not have the unlimited ownership of individual private property. Several differing groups have rights in the same corporate property. Stockholders, bondholders, and creditors have *investment rights*. They have a right to a return from funds placed at the disposal of the corporation. They are not, however, necessarily individual persons—they may be trust or pension funds, other corporations, or other organizational investors. Management actually administers the corporation and therefore has *control rights* over corporate assets. If a powerful minority bloc of stockholders is able to wrest control from management, its power is based not so much on stock holdings as on its position in the corporate power structure. Since the property of the corporation can be controlled through regulation by governmental bodies, it also is subject to *regulatory rights*. Finally, labor in its demands for job security is in effect claiming that it has *job rights* in corporate property. It is this fragmentation of corporate property that is the essence of the property revolution.

Despite the property revolution many people believe that the stockholder is in some sense an "owner" of the corporation. This is one of the myths of modern capitalism which we are reluctant to give up because it gives us security and reassurance in a rapidly changing world. We may not actually believe such a myth, but we act as though we do, probably because there is nothing to take its place. Votaw says of this myth: "Many people do not really believe it but are afraid not to. The lack of a substitute concept to provide legitimacy for the management, to supply control and restraint for the powerful and immortal corporate person, to support our belief in the democratic process, and to explain the nature of the modern corporation has made most of us reluctant to let go of the myth."[14] Perhaps the idea of the stockholder-owner can be better described as a legal fiction rather than a myth. We know that it is not true but we pretend to believe it because, after all, the system *does* work, and there might be disastrous consequences if we openly disavowed the concept.

In recent years there has been an attempt to support the legal fiction of the stockholder-owner by promoting the idea of "people's capitalism." The basis of this idea is the fact that more Americans own stock in corporations today than ever before (the New York Stock Exchange reports there were 17 million stockholders in 1962). Studies show, however, that the ownership of stock is concentrated in the hands of a small percentage of stockholders. Economist Robert Lampman estimates that the 1.6 percent of the adult population having a net worth of $60,000 or more held 82.4 percent of all publicly held shares of stock in 1953.[15] Therefore, the idea that there is widespread popular control over big business by stockholder-owners is unfounded.

What kind of an economic order can we have with the present pattern of property rights? Father Paul P. Harbrecht thinks that we are rapidly becoming a "paraproprietal society." By this term he means "a society beyond property." He believes that our society has passed from a property system to a power system, one in which ownership itself has less and less significance as an operating reality.[16] The same position is taken by Berle. He points to the rise of pension funds and the concentration of control of these funds in the hands of a few dozen giant banks and insurance companies.[17] On the whole, Harbrecht and Berle are rather optimistic about the situation. Although they have some misgivings about the uses to which pension fund trustees will put the wealth in their care, they do not foresee a collapse of the capitalistic system. Rather they see the development of a new "economic republic" that transcends old-style capitalism.

A much more pessimistic interpretation is given by James Burnham in his book *The Managerial Revolution*. He believes that the economic, social, political, and cultural institutions of the Western world are in a period of rapid transition. The movement is away from a social system dominated by capitalists to one dominated by managers. Burnham, formerly an avowed Communist, does not agree with Marx about the withering away of the state if private property were abolished. He argues that if capitalists are dispossessed by the property revolution, it does not follow that there will be no ruling class to take their place. "What is occurring in this transition is a drive for social dominance, for power and privilege, for the position of ruling class, by the social group or class of the managers."[18]

The property revolution is placed in the same concept of class struggle by various British writers. R. H. S. Crossman observes that "the main task of socialism today is to prevent the concentration of power in the hands either of industrial management or the state bureaucracy."[19] A pamphlet published by the British Labour party states, "It is not difficult to envisage a managerial caste taking on the former role of the owners of wealth and using its economic power to buttress class privileges and institutions."[20]

The Capitalist Revolution

The old capitalist morality was based on the classical economics idea that the natural force of competition dispenses a stern but equitable justice to all economic groups. The share of economic output received by each individual is based on his capacity to compete in the market. He gets what he deserves—according to the verdict of the market—not what he needs. This approach to income distribution is quite compatible with the Darwinian notion of "survival of the fittest." The logic of the classical economics seems inevitably to lead to the conclusion "that the health of society positively requires the weakest to go to the wall."[21] Those who do not contribute to the total store of goods available to the society cannot be subsidized without weakening the total system, it is implied. Therefore, it is unwise to educate the poor or give charity to those who cannot help themselves. Such well-meaning but misguided actions merely disturb the dynamic balance of society.

A new moral order of capitalism, one which utilizes new means to attain old ends, has been evolving in the United States in recent decades. As we have seen, the organizational, corporate, managerial, and property revolutions have transformed the basic institutions and doctrines of capitalism—private property, the profit motive, the market system, and *laissez faire*. These were the means to attain the original capitalistic ends of greater individual economic freedom, justice, and progress. The laissez-faire individualism of the old moral order has given way to the political interrelationships of organized economic interest groups. This does not imply that the individual no longer counts; it means only that alone and unaided he is incapable of defending himself in the organizational society. It is a paradox of our times that if the values of individualism are to flourish, the rights of individuals must be protected by organizations.

The capitalist revolution also consists of a reinterpretation of the ends of capitalism. Economic freedom no longer applies only to the business class, as it did in the eighteenth century when Manchester liberalism developed as a probusiness political reform movement. In the new moral order of capitalism, economic freedom is desired for all economic groups and classes, but it is defined differently. Economic freedom means being free from something that makes it difficult to make a living. In the eighteenth century the rising business class wanted to be free from the mercantilist restrictions imposed on them by government. Today, in our employee-oriented economy, the thing that most people fear is the loss of their jobs or the reduced income and standard of living brought on by a depression. Therefore, lapses from full employment are what they want to be free from. The government is now considered by most Americans to be a necessary instrument to attain sustained full employment; thus governmental intervention in the economy is a means to economic freedom rather than an obstacle to be overcome.

Another aspect of the capitalist revolution is the role played by government in maintaining a balance of power among interest groups. We now have a pluralistic power structure in which large and well-integrated groups represent the significant divisions of economic interests in the society. Business, labor, and agriculture compete with one another to further the interests of their members. This is the form that democratic processes logically would be expected to take in the organizational society. "In sociological terms, in fact, a democratic society can be defined as one in which no single occupational group, class, party, or other social segment holds substantial or long-sustained power over another or all others, either in intergroup relations or through the political process."[22] The government's role in the process is to act as an impartial umpire most of the time and to shore up the weaker groups when they are hard-pressed by the others. The influence wielded in this way can be of a highly moral as well as a political nature. For example, the Committee on Government Contracts puts pressure on companies throughout the nation to expand job opportunities for Negroes and Jews. The members of this committee operate, in effect, as a moral pressure group at the highest levels of government.

The capitalist revolution has led to a merging of public and private economic activity that is unprecedented in American history. The large corporation has a tendency today to perform functions that are essentially public in nature. An example is the corporation set up by Congress to operate the communications satellite system. The American Telephone and Telegraph Company is a partner in this venture along with the National Aeronautics and Space Administration and the Federal Communications Commission. The corporation has a board of three members appointed by the President, and it operates within guidelines specified by Congress in order to ensure operation in the public interest. It is not a public corporation like TVA because its stock is available to the public and to the communications carriers. Other examples of the close bond between the public and private spheres are the arrangements by which public agencies contract to have research and development work done by nongovernmental organizations; the full-time employment by government of individuals who remain on private salary; and the tendency of public regulatory commissions to promote the interests of the industries they are supposed to regulate in the public interest.

Thus the clear line of demarcation that previously could be drawn between the large private corporation and public agencies is becoming blurred. "Government has sought increasingly to use the private corporation for the performance of what are essentially public functions. Private corporations in turn . . . continually make decisions which impinge on the public . . . policy of government."[23] When this happens managers tend to take on the attitudes, motivations, goals, and administrative techniques of high-minded civil servants. This is another reason why the question of who owns the means of production in modern industrial society has lost much of its relevance. "The basic fact is the large corporation facing fundamentally similar problems, acts in fundamentally the same way, whether publicly or privately owned."[24]

The burden of public obligation has been thrust upon the corporation and management by the long-run contradictory forces of industrialization, which concentrates economic power, and democracy, which diffuses political power. In earlier societies, either the worker had freedom based on his ownership of the means of production (e.g., the agricultural economy of America in the eighteenth and early nineteenth centuries) or he had neither freedom nor property (e.g., slavery and feudalism). In mid-twentieth-century America, men are personally and politically free, but for the most part they are propertyless employees and economically dependent upon others who control their means of livelihood. They have instituted through political means certain safeguards against economic calamity, but there is no desire to completely collectivize economic life. To do so would go against the strong strain of individualism in the American character. The result is an economic system somewhere between *laissez faire* and total economic planning. One of the key characteristics of the system is its reliance upon informal mechanisms to ensure compatibility between private and public objectives, rather than the formal use of force as in communistic societies.

Undermining of the Profit Ethic

The five economic revolutions have led to a business and economic system in which the profit ethic is not operational for the large corporation. An operational business ethic, to be effective, must be based on a realistic appraisal of the social and political environment in which big business functions. If they are to develop an ethic upon which to base day-to-day decisions, managers must see things as they are, not as they would like to see them. And things as they are are not compatible with the single-minded pursuit of profit. Cooperation is gaining relative to competition in the organizational society; and politics, compared to economics, is making progress as a way of getting things done. The big-business corporation is becoming the key social institution in American society. There are so many purposes and facets to its activities that a simple goal of profit maximization is not practical. Managers now recognize that their social role is more complicated than that of the nineteenth-century captain of industry. They are expected to guide the corporation in fulfilling its manifold social obligations, not just to make as much money as possible for themselves or the stockholders. They are responsible to society at large in the employee-oriented society created by the property revolution. Managers and government officials, influenced strongly by customers and voters, are the ones who make big-business capitalism work, not natural laws of the universe.

Competition and cooperation are alternative ways to get things done in society. Competition motivates individuals to outdo each other in attaining scarce objects. Cooperation is a means whereby individuals can join forces to accomplish objectives beyond their individual capabilities. Both processes are found in some degree in every society. The balance between them depends upon the values, goals, and problems of the society. Competition was emphasized in the Age of Enterprise because it fitted the individualistic temperament of the American people and was helpful in attaining the goal of industrialization. The profit ethic was appropriate in such a competitive setting because it provided the motivation required to transform the economy. But there has been a shift in the organizational society from competition to cooperation. We now recognize how interdependent the elements of the economy are. Labor, management, government, agriculture, and the professions must cooperate to attain such goals as full employment and price stability. The profit ethic does not fit into a cooperative system as well as it does a competitive one. It is uncompromising, whereas what is needed is accomodation. Shifting the economic frame of reference from the market to the entire economic system has undermined the profit ethic because it is primarily a microeconomic concept whereas the focus of public policy today is on macroeconomic problems.

The increased importance of the political aspects of economic life has been criticized by Boulding. He finds little evidence that large-scale organizations have materially benefitted their members, but he argues that there are definite disadvantages to the shift from economic to political controls over business. He believes that the "unconscious and automatic coordination of human activity" through the market is vastly superior to the "conscious planning through instruments of authority and subordination" of political organizations.[25] Niebuhr, on the other hand, takes the position that the "politicization" of economic life is necessary to overcome the inequalities of power created by the rise of the big-business corporation.[26] Regardless of who is right, one thing stands out: The profit ethic is much more of an economic than a political concept. To the extent that there has been a politicization of economic life, the profit ethic has diminished in importance as an operational business ethic.

The transformation of the corporation from a producer of goods and services into a multipurpose social institution also has undermined the profit ethic. This transformation reverses the historical trend toward specialization of social structures. Primitive societies tend to have few social structures, and each one performs many different functions. The family, for example, may perform economic, educational, social, political, military, and religious functions. As societies become larger and more complex, social structures tend to specialize in function. As a social structure increases in size, it becomes unwieldy and it breaks down into separate components through the process of "structural differentiation," each part now becoming an independent structure.[27] The reverse has occurred in the case of the modern large corporation. It has taken on additional functions in society as it has grown larger. The profit ethic may have been an adequate guideline in decision making when the business firm was a specialist economic organization, but it is not up to the task of deciding between complex alternatives which affect the members of society in many different ways.

Businessmen have always been controlled by society in some way. The most comprehensive way to conceive of this system of control is to think of the businessman as the occupant of a social status. Associated with this status is a set of role expectations—what society expects the businessman to do. When he lives up to his expectations he is rewarded and when he does not he is punished. Profit making was the major expectation of the businessman role in the Age of Enterprise. But because of the different milieu in which the corporation operates and the different social role of the corporation, the role expectations of the modern manager go far beyond profit making, and they do not include profit maximization. A parallel can be drawn between the role expectations of managers and market structures. We used to think there were only two market structures—pure competition and monopoly. Consequently there were two ways to make decisions about price and output. Since the demonstration by Mrs. Robinson and Professor Chamberlin that there are various degrees of imperfection of markets, we have become aware of monopolistic competition and oligopoly and a variety of approaches to price and output decisions.[28] Now we are ready, perhaps, to see that just as there are other market structures so there are other legitimate business goals besides profit and thus other role expectations besides profit maximization.

NOTES

1 Kenneth E. Boulding, *The Organizational Revolution* (New York: Harper & Row, Publishers, Incorporated, 1953).

2 Robert A. Dahl and Charles E. Lindblom, *Politics, Economics, and Welfare* (New York: Harper & Row, Publishers, Incorporated, 1953), p. 235.

3 John William Ward, "The Ideal of Individualism and the Reality of Organization," in Earl F. Cheit (ed.), *The Business Establishment* (New York: John Wiley & Sons, Inc., 1964), pp. 37–76.

4 Peter F. Drucker, *Concept of the Corporation* (New York: The John Day Company, Inc., 1946), pp. 6, 7.

5 A. D. H. Kaplan, *Big Enterprise in a Competitive System* (Washington, D.C.: The Brookings Institution, 1954).

6 Norton Long, "The Corporation, Its Satellites, and the Local Community," in Edward S. Mason (ed.), *The Corporation in Modern Society* (Cambridge, Mass.: Harvard University Press, 1959), pp. 207–217.

7 Max Lerner, *America as a Civilization* (New York: Simon and Schuster, Inc., 1957), p. 311.

8 Dow Votaw, "The Mythology of Corporations," *California Management Review,* vol. 4, no. 3 (Spring, 1962), pp. 58–73.

9 The quotations in this paragraph are taken from Theodore Levitt, *The Twilight of the Profit Motive* (Washington, D.C.: Public Affairs Press, 1955), p. 1.

10 Peter F. Drucker, "Business Objectives and Survival Needs: Notes on a Discipline of Business Enterprise," *Journal of Business,* vol. 31, no. 2 (April, 1958), pp. 87–88.

11 *Ibid.,* pp. 85–86.

12 Robin M. Williams, Jr., *American Society* (New York: Alfred A. Knopf, Inc., 1957), p. 172.

13 Adolf A. Berle, Jr., and Gardiner C. Means, *The Modern Corporation and Private Property* (New York: The Macmillan Company, 1932), pp. 346–347.

14 Votaw, *op. cit.,* p. 64.

15 Robert J. Lampman, *Changes in the Share of Wealth Held by Top Wealth-holders, 1922–1956* (New York: National Bureau of Economic Research, Inc., 1960).

16 Paul P. Harbrecht, S.J., *Pension Funds and Economic Power* (New York: The Twentieth Century Fund, 1959).

17 Adolf A. Berle, Jr., *Power without Property* (New York: Harcourt, Brace & World, Inc., 1959).

18 James Burnham, *The Managerial Revolution* (Bloomington, Ind.: Indiana University Press, 1960), p. 71.

19 R. H. S. Crossman, *New Fabian Essays* (London: Turnstile Press, 1952), p. 27.

20 *Industry and Society* (London: British Labour party, 1957), p. 51.

21 J. Bronowski, *Darwinism and the Study of Society* (London: Tavistock Publications, 1961), p. xi.

22 Michael D. Reagan, *The Managed Economy* (Fair Lawn, N.J.: Oxford University Press, 1963), p. 179.

23 Mason, *op. cit.*, p. 16.

24 C. A. R. Crosland, *The Future of Socialism* (New York: St. Martin's Press, Inc., 1957), p. 480.

25 Kenneth E. Boulding, *The Organizational Revolution* (New York: Harper & Row, Publishers, Incorporated, 1953), p. 49.

26 Reinhold Niebuhr, "Coercion, Self-interest, and Love," *ibid.*, p. 230.

27 Neil J. Smelser, *Social Change in the Industrial Revolution* (Chicago: The University of Chicago Press, 1959), p. 2.

28 Joan Robinson, *The Economics of Imperfect Competition* (New York: St. Martin's Press, Inc., 1933); Edward Hastings Chamberlin, *The Theory of Monopolistic Competition* (Cambridge, Mass.: Harvard University Press, 1933).

The moral crisis in management

3
Life Cycle
of Business
Ethics

A business ethic may be radical, conservative, or reactionary with regard to the existing social order. There is a moral crisis in management today because the profit ethic is reactionary—it no longer fits the existing social order. This chapter traces the profit ethic through its life cycle and analyzes the present stage of development of the social responsibility ethic.

Definition of the Moral Crisis in Management

There is both an operational and an ideological aspect to any ethic. The operational aspect is a moral principle or guideline for practical decision making. Underlying it is an ideology—a belief system about the phenomenon calling for moral judgment. For example, the Ten Commandments is an operational ethic based on the Judeo-Christian conception of God, man, and the universe. The difference between the operational and ideological aspects of an ethic is the difference between action and belief. The individual acts (i.e., he makes decisions) in a certain way because he holds a particular set of beliefs.

Action does not always correspond to ideology, however. In fact, people often act in ways which are inconsistent with the ideologies they hold. An individual professing racial equality may choose to live in a neighborhood where there are no members of minority groups. A leading textbook of social problems takes the position that most social problems are caused by "nice people" who fail to live up to their laudable ideologies.[1]

Thus it is possible for an individual to employ an operational ethic in decision making that does not correspond to the ideological ethic in which he believes. When this happens he faces a moral crisis. He actually straddles two incompatible ethics. He counterpoises the operational aspect of one against the ideological aspect of another. He faces a moral crisis because he no longer can believe his view of the world is consistent with the moral principles that govern his behavior in it. To resolve the crisis he must change either his ideological system, the moral principle, or both, and make the operational and ideological aspects of the ethic consistent. These relationships are shown in the table. Conditions of moral crisis are AoBi and AiBo. There is no moral crisis in conditions AoAi and BoBi.

	ethic A	ethic B
Operational aspect	Ao	Bo
Ideological aspect	Ai	Bi

When we say there is a moral crisis in management, we mean that managers are using the operational ethic of social responsibility while believing in the ideology of the profit ethic. We take the position that this crisis will be resolved when the ideological ethic changes and conforms to the operational ethic. Social change in recent decades has led to a situation in which there are compelling reasons for managers to be socially responsible. But there is still strong ideological support of the profit ethic. It will be easier to accommodate ideology to the operational ethic of social responsibility than to remake the world to fit the ideology of the profit ethic. Therefore, the moral crisis in management will be resolved by a change in the ideological, rather than the operational aspect of business ethics.

Let us now turn to the question of why a gap developed between the operational and ideological aspects of business ethics.

Radical, Conservative, and Reactionary Business Ethics

Politically speaking, "An ideology is a program for organizing the resources, institutions, purposes, and power relations of society."[2] Every group in society has an ideology. The AFL-CIO has a labor ideology, the NAM has a business ideology, and the National Farmers' Union has a farm ideology. Each stresses the values, goals, and interests of the members of the group. When the existing social, political, and economic order is favorable for the protection and furtherance of a group's values, goals, and interests, it has a conservative ideology. The term "conservative" refers not to the content of the ideology but to its relation to prevailing institutions. A conservative ideology explains and defends existing institutions. A group which considers itself disadvantaged may have a revolutionary ideology which attacks existing institutional arrangements. Following a revolution a group which has lost ground may have a reactionary ideology that calls for a return to earlier institutional forms.

The ideology of a group is an important source of the solidarity of its members. By believing in the same things they are able to identify with each other, cooperate, protect common values, and work toward common goals. The ideology of a group may be so important to the integration of its members that ideological distortions of the real world become institutionalized. A source of distortion is the fact that "the members of a group need some sort of common cognitive orientation in order to cooperate; since social reality is complex, this common cognitive orientation is likely to be oversimplified from a scientific point of view."[3] The group regulates the ideology of its members to maintain solidarity. Sanctions are invoked against members of the group whose beliefs deviate substantially from the ideology. Through such social control, the norms of the group are maintained and a united front is mobilized against threats to the welfare of group members.

The business community is an interest group, and it strongly influences the ideological content of business ethics. It protects the prevailing ideological ethic against defections from within the ranks of business. Businessmen clearly are in a favorable position to influence adoption or rejection of new ideas about business and economics. Whether they support or oppose new ethical concepts will depend to a great extent on whether in their judgment those concepts will have a favorable or unfavorable effect on their own welfare. Thus the term "business community" refers to the largely unorganized vested interest group of business. There is a consensus in the business community regarding the ideological aspects of business ethics, and sanctions are invoked against any member of that community who deviates from them. Thus the ideological content of business ethics safeguards the interests of businessmen as a socioeconomic class.

An ideological business ethic is conservative (i.e., supports the status quo) when businessmen believe their interests are well served by the existing social order. The business community advocates a radical ideological business ethic when businessmen want to improve their situation in some way. When they believe the tide of social change is running against their best interests, businessmen back a reactionary ideological ethic.

All this has nothing to do with operational business ethics. Business practice changes over time in response to changes in technology and organization. Operational ethics necessarily are consistent with business practice because they arise out of day-to-day problems in running the firm's affairs (e.g., should the civil rights movement influence hiring practices, should industrial espionage be used, should a manufacturing process be automated if it results in unemployment). Whether it is implicit or explicit and well-thought-out or intuitive, whatever guideline is followed constitutes an operational ethic.

Ideological ethics, on the other hand, may be radical, conservative, or reactionary compared to business practice and the operational ethic. Historically, the profit ethic has passed through all three phases: In the Industrial Revolution it was radical; in the Age of Enterprise it was conservative; today it is reactionary. The social responsibility ethic is presently radical. When it becomes conservative in the future, there no longer will be a moral crisis in management.

The Profit Ethic as Radical during the Industrial Revolution

The most central social problem in the modern era is the question of the proper relation between the individual and the state. Social, political, and economic life were organized around the institutions of feudalism following the breakup of the Roman Empire. The tight local organization of feudal life provided a semblance of social order, but in return the individual accepted massive restrictions on his freedom of action. Two forces, both associated with the decline of feudalism, led to a change in the relation of the individual to social structure. The first was the rise of the modern nation-state. Toward the end of the Middle Ages, monarchs began to assert their authority over the feudal nobles. The Reformation supported this development by diverting part of the personal allegiance of the mass of citizens from the church to the king. The second, the Renaissance from the fall of Constantinople to the end of the seventeenth century, emphasized the moral and political autonomy of the individual. The concept of the "masterless man" gained popularity as men recognized their individuality and came to value it. The conflict between personal autonomy and the authority of the state to which these forces inevitably led is still with us today.

The middle class which began to develop following the breakup of feudalism was initially under the control of the landed nobility. It entered into an alliance with the kings, who desired to crush the independence and autonomous powers of their dukes and counts. Thus the rise of the middle class was a by-product of the rise of absolute monarchy. As the kings of England and France rose above the other nobles, the middle class gained its freedom from the nobles but became servants of the king. Modern capitalism developed in England under royal control during the sixteenth and seventeenth centuries. Businessmen had more freedom than in the thirteenth-century town, but they had to operate in an economy which was strictly regulated by the royal government. "Far from leaving the economy to its own working, the royal governments tried to extend over *the whole country* a system of control in many ways similar to that of the medieval city."[4]

This was mercantilism, the most influential economic policy and doctrine of the seventeenth and eighteenth centuries. The goal of mercantilism was to make the state as independent, self-sufficient, and powerful as possible. Mercantilism was never a unified policy or doctrine. Rather it was a shifting combination of tendencies directed at a common aim—the increase of national power. The core of mercantilism was the strengthening of the state in material resources. Thus mercantilism was the economic side of nationalism. Schmoller hit the mark when he said the essence of mercantilism was "state-making." By this he meant the creation of an economic community out of the political community:[5]

> The essence of the system lies not in some doctrine of money, or of the balance of trade; not in tariff barriers, protection duties, or navigation laws; but in something far greater:—namely, in the total transformation of society and its organization, as well as of the state and its institutions, in the replacing of a local and territorial economic policy by that of the national state.

In mercantilism the individual was unconditionally subordinated to the state. He was not regarded as an end in himself, but as a tool for implementing state aims. This was as true of the businessman as anyone else. He was expected to work toward the welfare of the nation. Collective economic goals took precedence over individual ones. This was rationalized on the ground that the welfare of the individual depends upon the security he is provided by the state. Thus social order was viewed as the cause of individual freedom.

In England there was a general belief among the merchants that they were sacrificed to state interests. The underlying idea, according to Eli Heckscher, the leading historian of mercantilism, was that "the profit of the merchant in itself was no criterion of the profit of the country, but on the contrary, the profit of the individual could be the country's loss and vice versa."[6] Thomas Mun, a leading mercantilist writer, distinguished between the commercial gain of the country, the merchant, and the king, and pointed out the possibility that any one of the three could realize a profit while the other two suffered losses.[7] Josiah Child, a contemporary of Mun's, pictured the merchants as martyrs of society. He started with the premise that "all Trade will be less gainful to Individuals, though more profitable to the Public," and wondered, "whatever becomes of the poor merchants."[8]

Thus there was implicit in mercantilist thought a dichotomy between the welfare of the individual and the state. One did not necessarily lead to the other. Where there was a conflict between the two, the welfare of the state prevailed.

The stage was set for the decline of mercantilism by the Industrial Revolution in the late eighteenth and early nineteenth centuries. This revolution occurred in three phases: (1) changes in manufacturing and transportation, made possible by the development of power-driven machinery; (2) the shift from small-scale production in the home to large-scale production in the factory; and (3) changes in social organization brought on by the new production techniques and the factory system. The Industrial Revolution originated in Great Britain, leaped across the English Channel to France after the Napoleonic Wars, and was introduced later in Germany and the Scandinavian countries.

It was not by chance that this revolution commenced in England. The feudal system and the medieval preoccupation with the life hereafter declined more rapidly there than on the continent. An ideological system developed which was conducive to individual freedom and fairly rapid social and economic mobility. This was manifested in economic life by the early decline of serfdom and the guild system and the emergence of a manufacturing system based on handicrafts and petty capitalism. The medieval customs barriers between towns and regions were abolished early, and the social climate was favorable for trade. Social and political conditions were propitious for the rise of a new business class. Thus long before the appearance of the technological innovations which gave the Industrial Revolution its initial impetus, ideological and organizational conditions were ripe for such a development.

One of the most notable changes in social organization brought on by the Industrial Revolution was the rise of a new business class. Many men of humble origin got ahead by grasping opportunities provided by the new technology and industry. Many of them left farming to establish small factories to produce cotton, iron, or pottery. The entrepreneurs rarely were engineers or inventors, but they were tireless advocates of the innovations of others. They were willing to take risks, and they had great energy and boundless ambition. Eventually the successful entrepreneurs who made up the new business class became so wealthy and influential that they were able to challenge the authority of the members of the landed gentry who had traditionally governed England.

The members of the new business class became increasingly restive under the mercantilist restrictions of their activities as the pressure mounted to expand manufacturing and foreign trade. Businessmen advocated the abolition of tariffs and other regulations governing foreign trade. They argued that England could only benefit from free trade because it had the highest level of industrialization in Europe. For a time their pleas went unheeded. Members of the landowning class supported mercantilist policies, and they were still powerful in Parliament. The businessmen wanted to take the economy out from under the domination of the state so that it could function according to its own natural laws. Their demands were in keeping with broad currents of social change of the times, but to realize them the business class first had to gain political concessions from the landowners. A social philosophy was needed which called for a new relation between the state and the economy, and between government and the individual.

Classical liberalism was such a philosophy. It valued progress over tradition and competition over harmony. It was peace loving, democratic, and equalitarian, and it had an immense respect for private property. Classical liberals had a bias against government and feared that its powers would be used illegitimately. They believed the government's functions should be limited to the protection of individual liberty. In short, classical liberalism suited the businessman's need for a social philosophy which offered a new definition of the productive relations between men. It was the product of a way of thinking in which business values were more central than social, political, religious, or military considerations.

The most outspoken advocates of the new philosophy were the members of the Manchester School of liberals. They were businessmen in the Manchester area who urged that mercantilism be immediately discarded and replaced with *laissez faire*. They took over the term *laissez faire* from the Physiocrats, a group in France who also wanted to apply liberal ideas to economics. The cry of the Physiocrats, *"Laissez nous faire, laissez nous passer!"* ("Leave us alone to produce what we want and to send our products where we want!"), was shortened to *"Laissez faire!"*: "Leave us alone!" This is exactly what the Manchester liberals wanted. They argued that all relations between individuals should be based on mutual free consent rather than coercion by the state. They stressed the importance of individual freedom in economic affairs, and they believed the state's role in the economy should be limited to the maintenance of law and order. Like the Physiocrats, they argued that the economic activities of buying, selling, and consuming should be completely free, because they are controlled by natural rather than man-made laws.

The free trade argument of the Manchester liberals received theoretical support from Adam Smith and other members of the classical school of economics. Smith observed the gradual decline of the mercantilist system of national economic planning in the late eighteenth century. Individual initiative of businessmen was becoming a mass phenomenon for the first time in history, but business was still hampered by remaining mercantilist restrictions and regulations. Smith believed that control of individual behavior by the state was not in the best interests of the nation or the individual. He put forth the modern view that mutual dependence of nations leads to progress and is not detrimental to their welfare as the mercantilists thought. He argued that restrictions on manufacturing and foreign trade check the growth of a nation's wealth and impoverish its people.

The classical economists deduced how the capitalistic economy functions on the basis of the assumptions of natural law, universal competition, "economic man," and harmony of interests. Their analysis was centered around the four economic institutions of private property, the profit motive, the market system, and *laissez faire.* Private property was considered fundamental because it gives the businessman control over economic resources and it serves as an incentive for the accumulation of wealth. The profit motive leads the businessman to expand the output of goods consumers want and to cut back production of less desirable goods. The economic system consists of self-regulating markets which match the supply and demand of goods. Competition in markets sets prices and thereby controls indirectly the activities of buyers and sellers. *Laissez faire* is essential for the forces of the market to allocate resources efficiently and for individuals to effectively pursue their self-interest.

A new business ethic was needed for the burgeoning capitalistic system, and the profit ethic evolved quite naturally to fill this need. Technology, organization, and business practices had changed so markedly as a result of the Industrial Revolution that the mercantilist view of how businessmen should behave was now quite reactionary. Businessmen advocated the concept of profit maximization as a replacement. It offered them a radical new basis for deciding between morally right and wrong conduct. Businessmen defended the flotation of Russian state bonds in the London stock exchange during the height of the Crimean War on the basis of this new ethic. They argued that there is no relation between foreign policy and the laws of economic life, and therefore it would be foolish not to take advantage of a profitable bit of business. There could have been no sharper rejection of the economic policy and doctrine of mercantilism.

This radical viewpoint became acceptable to social thought in nineteenth-century Great Britain, largely because of the success of capitalism in raising living standards. Herbert Spencer, the most influential social philosopher of his day, shaped this thought by applying Darwin's theory of evolution to social life. He argued that ruthless competition is the basic law of industrial society. Those who win the economic race earn great profits and accumulate wealth, and the less fit share what is left. Spencer believed that anyone who cannot compete in the completely unregulated capitalistic system should not be allowed to survive and weaken the human stock. From this way of looking at things, the good man is the one who pursues profits most assiduously, and his social value is proportionate to his material success.

Classical economic theory supported the profit ethic in two ways: (1) by providing a scientific explanation of capitalism in which the profit motive plays a central role and (2) by defending capitalism and profit making on moral grounds. The classical economists thought mercantilism was wrong because it was opposed to the scientific truth that competition among individuals for scarce goods in free markets is the natural law of economic life. They believed that if all restraints were removed on man's inherent desire to maximize profits, natural resources would seek their most profitable and efficient employment. The profit maximization hypothesis was not only morally justified; it was essential to a theory that purported to predict price, wage, and employment levels, the allocation of resources, and the distribution of income. Mason has pointed out the dual nature of the classical economics as both science and justification of ideology: "As everyone now recognizes, classical economics provided not only a system of analysis . . . but also a defense . . . of the proposition that the economic behavior promoted and constrained by the institutions of a free-enterprise system is, in the main, in the public interest."9

The Profit Ethic as Conservative in the Age of Enterprise

The profit ethic was accepted readily in America during the 1880s and 1890s. Industrial capitalism emerged triumphant in this period. America was transformed into an urban and industrial society. Changes brought about in the economy by industrialization were transmitted to every other area of life. The entrepreneurs who led in the march into industrialism were national folk heroes. Business values and objectives attained an all-time high of social acceptance. It was generally agreed that the business of America was to create wealth. This orientation led to an emphasis on materialism unparalleled in America, either before or since the Age of Enterprise. Materialistic values were so strongly in evidence that Mark Twain called this era the Gilded Age.

The Industrial Revolution began in America at about the beginning of the nineteenth century. Merchants who had prospered during the wars between England and France supplied much of the capital to build factories. The infant industries which grew up were protected from foreign competition by European wars and protective tariffs. Railroad construction in the 1840s and 1850s and the Civil War in the 1860s stimulated manufacturing tremendously and laid the foundation for large-scale industrial activity in the Age of Enterprise. Men who were to later become the captains of industry—J. P. Morgan, Andrew Carnegie, and John D. Rockefeller, among others—established the basis of their fortunes and corporate and financial empires during the war. Following the war manufacturers rapidly expanded output to supply a national market swollen by immigration, a market that grew from 25 million people in 1850 to over 60 million in 1890.

The captains of industry deserve much of the credit for the rapid rate of industrialization in the Age of Enterprise. They were a hard-driving, daring, and ambitious group of men. They were not as polished as the managers of today, either in their manners or ethics. They tended to be crude, grasping, and egocentric. On the other hand, they were important agents of change. Without them, America would never have been able to accomplish its miracle of industrialization so rapidly. Therefore, it is not fair to call these men "robber barons." They operated in a period when a vast continent was being organized into a complicated industrial complex. Society set no rules for them to follow in this endeavor, so they made up their own as they went along.

A peculiar version of *laissez faire* prevailed in America during the Age of Enterprise: that government should not regulate or control business in any way but should do whatever possible to aid business. Tariff policy after the Civil War was extremely favorable to business. A series of tariff acts increased the average wartime rate of duties to 47 percent by 1864. This was supposed to be a temporary wartime measure, but tariffs were pushed even higher by the McKinley Act of 1890, the Dingley Act of 1897, and the Payne-Aldrich Act of 1909. Government also aided business by grants of land and other natural resources. The railroads were given 158 million acres of land, and large lumber companies circumvented the Homestead Act to gain control of valuable timber lands. The government also aided business by refraining from setting up regulatory commissions, by not passing legislation to protect labor, and by placing little or no restriction upon the uninhibited exploitation of economic opportunities by the captains of industry and financial tycoons.

Cultural values, social thought, and business practices reflected the rampant materialism of the day. Ideas about religion and morality lost influence, and some religious leaders began to justify the acquisition of wealth on religious grounds. The desire to win wealth led to excessive speculation, waste, and dishonesty. No attention was paid to conservation of resources. Get-rich-quick schemes abounded. Business ethics were lax. Few entrepreneurs felt the need of being completely honest. Sharp and unscrupulous competitive tactics went unpunished by society. The most notorious business practices of the day were the stock manipulations, the fleecing of railroads, and the cornering of markets by financial operators such as Jim Fiske, Jay Gould, and Daniel Drew.

American economists made no major contribution to the nineteenth-century literature of classical economics. They continued to teach the same classical doctrines, although they had little application to the dynamic economic processes that were leading America into the age of big business.

Lionel Robbins has pointed out that it is an oversimplification to think that the British classical economists were united in their view; all of them did not press *laissez faire* to its ultimate limit. They explored the alternative choices for a democratic society and prescribed policy over a wide range, depending upon their individual views of the appropriate balance to be struck between individual freedom and economic order.[10] American economic writing, on the other hand, tended to be political in nature, more along the line of ideological pamphleteering than sober scientific analysis.

The moral case for the profit ethic was made most clearly by Andrew Carnegie in his "gospel of wealth." John Bates Clark, an American economist who was a contemporary of Carnegie's, had popularized classical economic theory as the science of wealth. Carnegie, an intelligent and morally preoccupied man, emphasized the moral dimension of the same subject in his gospel. There were two sources of the gospel of wealth, one derived from religious ideas and the other from a scientific approach to the study of man. The former was based on the idea of the divine nature of property. Since the Creator intended that man acquire property and hang on to it, so the argument went, property rights derived from a higher authority than man-made laws. Spencer's application to society of Darwin's theory of evolution was the second source of the gospel of wealth. On the basis of Spencer's work, Carnegie argued that it is a dog-eat-dog world. The strong survive and prosper, and the weak eke out a bare existence and many of them fall by the wayside. Carnegie was careful to point out, however, that a rich man's wealth is a sacred trust put into his hand by God to be administered for the welfare of society.

Thus there was no gap between ideological business ethics and operating business ethics and business practice in the Age of Enterprise. The ideological basis of the profit ethic had early immigrated to the New World. Almost from the start Americans were highly individualistic and materialistic in outlook. Once the technological competence and the capital needed to develop the factory system were available, it was a forgone conclusion that industrialization would occur. The businessman was in the ascendant economically and politically practically as soon as there was any business community in America. The profit ethic, far from being radical as it had been early in the Industrial Revolution, was strongly supportive of the status quo. And in turn it was supported by the deepest social values and religious impulses of the day. Never in the history of the world has the social environment been so hospitable to the free play of the spirit of free enterprise as it was in the Age of Enterprise.

The Profit Ethic as Reactionary Today

The collapse of the economy in 1929 led to a train of events which has rendered pure and unadulterated profit maximization obsolete and reactionary as an operating business ethic. It soon became clear in the miserable years of the early 1930s that the classical economists' notion that there could be no deep and long-lasting depression was wrong. The economy was all too clearly not self-regulating. Thus the support which the profit ethic had received from classical economic theory eroded away. Its other ideological support, *laissez faire,* was utterly demolished by the New Deal.

Since the 1930s the business community has experienced its share of reverses in the maneuvering for political advantage in the modern general-welfare state. Businessmen have developed appropriate operational ethics for the new milieu in which they operate, but they have been at a loss when it comes to an ideological interpretation of the new status quo. They have come to believe that whatever direction the new dispensation is taking it is one not favorable to the interests of the business community. They hold on to the profit ethic as a symbol of all that they think business has lost.

The Great Depression and New Deal undermined the profit ethic by cutting the ground from under *laissez faire.* Since the days of the New Deal, it has been clear to everyone that the government plays a major role in control and regulation of the economy. Businessmen at first blamed New Deal intervention in the economy on Roosevelt, and they looked forward to the day when prosperity would return and government interference would cease. But successive administrations, including that of Eisenhower, have not reduced the level of government participation in the economy, despite the unprecedented prosperity of the post-World War II period.

It has now become clear that the New Deal was the manifestation in the United States of a worldwide reaction against laissez-faire capitalism.

Despite its long list of triumphs, there were strains developing in capitalism in the early twentieth century. One such strain was inequality of income distribution based on property rights. Another was the instability of capitalism. Dissatisfaction with capitalism, which previously had been latent, became overwhelming in the 1930s. The concept of the market as the only coordinating mechanism of economic activity was rejected. The capitalist world did not follow Russia's lead, however, and get rid of capitalistic institutions altogether. It moved toward some form of "mixed system" in which *laissez faire* had little or no part to play.

Classical economic theory was dealt a blow by the Great Depression from which it has not recovered. According to that theory there can be no long-lasting depression because "supply creates its own demand." According to Say's law there is always a sufficient rate of spending to maintain full employment. Money which people save from their income is channeled into investment uses by the interest rate. The theory was elegant, precise, and logical; but as often happens with beautiful theories, it was strangled by some brute facts. There was a depression! The discrepancy between theory and reality stimulated John Maynard Keynes to develop a new theory to refute the classical economics.[11] He reasoned that there is no necessary reason why the capitalist economy operates at full employment. It can just as well be in a slump for a protracted period. The key to full employment is an adequate level of income. If consumption plus investment spending is not great enough to fully employ economic resources, the only way to attain full employment is for the government to make up the difference through deficit spending. Keynes's theory is today the basis of monetary and fiscal policy in the nations of the free world.

The demise of the ideology of *laissez faire* and the decline of classical economic theory have weakened the acceptance by the general public of the profit ethic. Businessmen are acutely aware of this. They complain that "profit has become a dirty word." In a way it has. There appears to be a good deal of suspicion of the motives of businessmen and a reluctance to place the responsibility for the economic welfare of the nation into their hands. The outcry when Charles Wilson said a few years ago that he had always believed that what was good for General Motors was good for America is a case in point. There seems to be a growing distaste for careers in business among students in the finest universities (e.g., in a recent graduating class at Harvard as many students were entering the Peace Corps as were going into business). People who are not members of the business community and who have no ideological axes to grind recognize that we are living in a different economic era than existed before the Great Depression and New Deal. A recent survey of economic attitudes of high school students indicated that they believe the government has responsibility for creating jobs and maintaining full employment. This shocks many businessmen, but as a matter of objective fact, the government's actions support the students' view.

Why, then, does the business community cling to the profit ethic when it has lost the popular support it once had? The reason is a political one. The New Deal brought about a reorganization of the political power of the various economic interest groups. Previously the business community had enjoyed practically a monopoly of this power. When the Supreme Court gave the corporation the status of a legal person, it gave business a powerful competitive advantage over other economic groups. As a result of the New Deal, the courts gave unions the same protection and immunities against legislative and executive controls which are guaranteed individuals under the Fifth and Fourteenth Amendments. Agriculture has also improved its political position since the New Deal. It now has one of the strongest lobbies in Washington. The result is that the business community has lost some of its political power to labor and agriculture. Consequently businessmen who have a strong feeling for free enterprise ideology believe that America is going down the primrose path of socialism. They believe that economic freedom is disappearing in America. What actually has happened, of course, is there has been a redistribution of the total amount of economic freedom among the major economic interest groups with no necessary decrease in the total.[12]

Business has seldom been more profitable than it is today. Yet businessmen are apprehensive. They feel that things are not as they should be. The difficulty they sense has nothing to do with "the facts." It is a product of ideological distortion of changes in the power structure. When faced with a changed environment, one in which the *relative* political position of the business community is weakened, it is easy for businessmen to conclude that the future is dangerous. Thus they continue to believe in the profit ethic which was so gloriously in tune with the march of events in the great days of the 1880s and 1890s. The Age of Enterprise stands for them as the high watermark of American progress and economic sanity.

To be fair to the business community, it must be noted that it has received precious little help from academics and other intellectuals in developing an ideology that is congruent with the contemporary scene. Most economists, for example, are still quite committed to the profit ethic because of the key role it plays in their model building.[13] We have moved so rapidly toward a unique combination of private and public economic institutions in the past few decades that the old dichotomy between capitalism and socialism has lost much of its meaning. What we need today is a new ideology to replace *laissez faire* and a new economic theory to complement the classical economics. When our ideology builders and economic theorists provide these, businessmen will have an alternative to which to turn. Then they will no longer be forced to worship a dead ideology while helping to forge the new world which killed it.

Managerial Ideology and the Social Responsibility Ethic

Thus far we have treated the business community as a monolith, as if all businessmen held the same ideology. Clearly this has never been the case, but as long as there was a high degree of consensus and the business community did not break up into distinct ideological camps, such a view was a useful approximation. This no longer is true. Today there are two separate and fairly well-defined business ideologies: the classical business ideology and the managerial business ideology. The classical ideology is the foundation of the profit ethic and the managerial ideology is the foundation of the social responsibility ethic. The managerial ideology is advocated by a minority of businessmen, but they are the leaders of the largest and most powerful corporations. They have fomented much of the controversy about business ethics (and helped bring about the moral crisis in management) by bringing forcefully to public attention the concept of socially responsible management. The majority of busimen still pay allegiance to the classical business ideology and the profit ethic, however, and therefore the social responsibility ethic is still in its radical phase.

The theory of strains and ideology developed by Francis Sutton and his colleagues in *The American Business Creed* helps to explain the rise of the managerial ideology. The general framework of their theory is stated in the following propositions:[14]

1 By far the greater part of human action is performed unreflectively.

2 The roots of this normal unreflectiveness lie in the very nature of societies and the way in which they mold the personalities of their members. No society simply presents its members with a random set of choices of possible behavior; it indicates the approved ways, and rewards or punishes as these are adopted or rejected.

3 Fortunately or unfortunately, societies and personalities are never completely free from difficulties and disturbances. . . . Individuals living in societies experience these imperfections as *strains;* they must at times face situations where the expectations they have learned to view as legitimate are thwarted, or where they must wrestle with conflicting demands.

4 Strains are "normal" in any society.

5 The strains to which the members of a particular society are subject do not simply vary at random; they are patterned.

6 The reactions to a given strain are not entirely random.

7 Ideology is a patterned reaction to the patterned strains of a social role.

Sutton et al. think the content of a business ideology can best be explained in terms of the strains which businessmen experience in playing their role. "Businessmen adhere to their particular kind of ideology because of the emotional conflicts, the anxieties, and the doubts engendered by the actions which their roles as businessmen compel them to take, and by the conflicting demands of other social roles which they must play in family and community."[15] The ideology attempts to resolve these conflicts, alleviate these anxieties, and overcome these doubts within the limits of what is publicly acceptable in the American cultural tradition.

A reasonable explanation of the cause of the managerial ideology is the strain engendered in the manager role by the conflict between the operating ethic of social responsibility and the ideological ethic of profit maximization. The source of ideological business ethics is ideas about what the business community thinks should be expected of the businessman. These ideas tend to be concrete, inflexible, "practical," doctrinaire, and dogmatic. On the other hand, the source of operational business ethics is what society expects of the businessman. At any moment of time, the direction in which society is moving is apt to be uncertain. "It is part of the burden of management that it must forever follow the uneven and winding trail of social consensus. Because social change is a more or less permanent condition and management is by temperament and social necessity conservative, there will always be strain in the management role."[16] When a new status quo is established and it is clear what society expects of managers, they adapt their behavior to the new situation and develop an appropriate ideology so that the level of strain in the manager role can be reduced to a tolerable level.

The emergence of the ethic of social responsibility can be explained by the need for managers to develop a more appropriate ideology for the contemporary scene than the laissez-faire–free enterprise–profit ethic approach. The leadership in developing the ethic has come from the top managers of the largest corporations. Such men as Theodore Houser of Sears, Roebuck, Ralph Cordiner of General Electric, Frank Abrams of Standard Oil of New Jersey, Clarence Randall of Inland Steel, David Rockefeller of the Chase Manhattan Bank, and Crawford Greenewalt of Du Pont have led the way in emphasizing the social responsibilities of big business and its leaders. They are the ones most likely to experience strain in the manager role because of conflict between ideological and operational business ethics. The great power they wield is subject to elusive but nonetheless definite social constraints—what Adolf Berle calls the public consensus: "the existence of a set of ideas, widely held by the community, and often by the organization itself and the men who direct it, that certain uses of power are 'wrong,' that is, contrary to the established interest and value system of the community."[17] A conflict between ideological and operational business ethics grows more or less spontaneously out of the day-to-day interaction of operating requirements and the public consensus. Its significance is not likely to be lost on top management. The strain generated by this conflict probably reached a point where it became necessary to develop a managerial ideology as a measure of psychological self-protection.

This explanation of the rise of the ethic of social responsibility is supported by the analysis of the difference between the managerial and classical versions of the American business creed by Sutton and his colleagues.

> The classical strand centers around the model of a decentralized, private, competitive capitalism, in which the forces of supply and demand, operating through the price mechanism, regulate the economy in detail and in aggregate. The managerial strand differs chiefly in the emphasis

it places on the role of professional managers in the large business firm who consciously direct economic forces for the common good.[18]

These two versions are quite different in fundamental conception, probably because big-business managers experience the conflict between ideological and operational business ethics much more directly than small businessmen who are more likely to be subject to the constraint of price competition.

What is necessary for the social responsibility ethic to move from the radical to the conservative phase of its life cycle? This requires changes in the way that businessmen perceive the business world rather than changes in the business world itself. Social change takes place in technology, organization, and ideology. The technological and organizational changes which led to the rise of big business modified the structure of market capitalism to such an extent that the social and economic mechanisms which the profit ethic depended upon for its rationale and legitimacy do not operate as effectively as before. New methods of operating have developed, but there has not been a corresponding shift in ideology. As the tension caused by the gap between ideology and technology and organization mounts, there will be a greater willingness to modify ideology. When the business community and the public have an economic ideology that fits the current economic scene, the social responsibility ethic will be compatible with it and will be in its conservative phase.

NOTES

1   John F. Cuber and Robert A. Harper, *Problems of American Society: Values in Conflict* (New York: Holt, Rinehart and Winston, Inc., 1948).

2   M. Morton Auerbach, *The Conservative Illusion* (New York: Columbia University Press, 1959), p. 6.

3   Harry Johnson, *Sociology* (New York: Harcourt, Brace & World, Inc., 1960), p. 593.

4   Eugene O. Golob, *The "Isms": A History and Evaluation* (New York: Harper & Row, Publishers, Incorporated, 1954), p. 5.

5   Gustav Schmoller, *The Mercantile System* (New York: St. Martin's Press, Inc., 1895), p. 51.

6   Eli Heckscher, *Mercantilism* (London: George Allen & Unwin, Ltd., 1935), p. 321.

7   Thomas Mun, *England's Treasure by Forraign Trade* (Oxford: Basil Blackwell & Mott, Ltd., 1949), chap. 7.

8   Josiah Child, *New Discourse of Trade* (London: T. Sowle, 1698), quoted in Heckscher, *op. cit.*, p. 321.

9   Edward S. Mason, "The Apologetics of 'Managerialism,' " *Journal of Business,* vol. 31, no. 1 (January, 1958), p. 5.

10 Lionel Robbins, *The Theory of Economic Policy* (New York: The Macmillan Company, 1952).

11 John Maynard Keynes, *The General Theory of Employment, Interest and Money* (New York: Harcourt, Brace & World, Inc., 1936).

12 Thomas A. Petit, *Freedom in the American Economy* (Homewood, Ill.: Richard D. Irwin, Inc., 1964).

13 Thomas D. Curtis, "The Function of Profit Maximization in Economic Models," *Arizona Review*, vol. 15, no. 2 (February, 1966), pp. 18–19.

14 Francis X. Sutton, Seymour E. Harris, Carl Kaysen, and James Tobin, *The American Business Creed* (Cambridge, Mass.: Harvard University Press, 1956), pp. 305–308.

15 *Ibid.,* p. 11.

16 Thomas A. Petit, "Management Ideology: Myth and Reality," *California Management Review,* vol. 3, no. 2 (Winter, 1961), p. 101.

17 Adolf A. Berle, Jr., *Power without Property* (New York: Harcourt, Brace & World, Inc., 1959), p. 90.

18 Sutton et al., *op. cit.*, pp. 33–34.

The Doctrine
of Social
Responsibility

Social thought about the obligation to society of business and businessmen has changed during the period in which the five revolutions were transforming capitalistic economy and society. We have moved from the principle that individual businessmen who have earned great profits are trustees of the nation's wealth toward the concept that the professional manager's duty to society lies in the way in which he actually operates the giant enterprise. Only in the post-World War II period has the doctrine of social responsibility been formulated clearly enough for its significance to become widely recognized and discussed. Most writings about the doctrine have been polemical, either strongly affirming or denying the existence, validity, and importance of the social responsibilities of corporate managers. On the whole, the critics of the doctrine have been more articulate than its supporters. Nonetheless the doctrine has gained steadily in stature.

Support of the Doctrine

Social thinkers who address themselves to the problems of modern industrial society can hardly avoid dealing explicitly or implicitly with the issue of the role of the corporation in modern society and the social responsibilities of management. Elton Mayo, Peter Drucker, Adolf Berle, and John Maynard Keynes have analyzed these matters. Their approaches differ in many ways but they agree on two basic points: (1) Industrial society faces serious human and social problems brought on largely by the rise of the large corporation, and (2) managers must conduct the affairs of the corporation in ways to solve or at least ameliorate these problems. Although their analyses do not deal specifically with the doctrine of socially responsible management, they implicitly offer powerful support for it.

Mayo rediscovered in the course of the Hawthorne experiments something psychologists had long known: that individuals are happiest and most comfortable when they are members of a primary group. He thought modern industrial society faces social disorganization because of "the breakdown of social codes that formerly disciplined us to effective working together."[1] Industrial society destroys the group solidarity of the church, small community, and guild. At the same time, it increases the number of pressure groups. The only way to achieve group solidarity and avoid chaos in industrial society is for the leaders of society—the managers—to employ human relations actively in industry. Human relations properly used could be a substitute in industrial society for the "simple religious feeling of medieval times."[2] The manager's function, according to Mayo, is to combine men into a modern counterpart of the tribe, clan, or guild in order to save society. A primary function of the business enterprise is to provide the basis for social order in industrial society.

Drucker considers democratic capitalism to have failed because it did not develop a functioning society (i.e., one which gives to each individual a status based on the social function he performs). Such a society existed in the Middle Ages, when to be a serf, guild member, or knight was to occupy a definite status based on a particular social function. Capitalism was able to be a functioning society only as long as it could make wealth and property the basis of prestige and status and was able to integrate men through the market system. The rise of the corporation and the consequent decline in the power of the market have made it impossible for modern society to be a functioning society, according to Drucker. The corporation is now the basic socioeconomic institution, rather than the feudal manor or the capitalistic market. Now that we have learned the secret of mass production, the task, as Drucker sees it, is to build a new functioning society that is compatible with the large corporation. The way to do this, he believes, is to make the industrial-plant community the basis of social as well as economic organization.[3]

Berle points out that since an economy is a means to an end rather than an end in itself, the way in which it is organized and functions is largely dependent upon the value system of the society in which it is embedded. The Protestant ethic was the great driving value system that propelled the American economy in the nineteenth century. Most definitions of this ethic stress the point of view which held private property sacred and hard work virtuous and which acclaimed thrift, accumulation, and independence. But Berle emphasizes the impersonal and selfless love which motivated men imbued with the Protestant ethic. "Thou shalt love thy neighbor as thyself" was its guiding principle. Men taxed themselves, developed social institutions such as social security and pension funds, and gave their personal wealth for motives independent of profit and exchange. Yet such actions led to capital accumulation and other results which have proved of inestimable value to purely self-interest commercial operations. Berle thus turns upside down Adam Smith's idea that economic man in pursuing his own selfish gain cannot help but further social goals. Berle thinks the individual who selflessly contributes to human and community betterment thereby strengthens its economic potential and directly benefits from the higher level of economic progress which results.[4]

Keynes believed that the best way to develop a stable, just, and free industrial society is to place our trust in the evolution of the existing structures of government and business, rather than to embrace a new and all-encompassing "ism" of some kind. He believed that the corporation is a type of economic entity which is sympathetic to the institutions of a free society. But by "corporation" he meant a type of semiautonomous public body—the universities, the Bank of England, the Port of London Authority, and the railway companies—rather than the typical business enterprise. He suggested, therefore, that private business enterprises take on the characteristics of such public service corporations. The criterion of action of such organizations would be solely the public good as they understood it. Keynes did not think that his views were naïvely utopian, and as proof of their practicality pointed to the trend of big business to socialize itself:[5]

> A point arrives in the growth of a big institution—particularly a big railway or big public utility enterprise, but also a big bank or a big insurance company—at which the owners of the capital, i.e., the shareholders, are almost entirely dissociated from the management, with the result that the direct personal interest of the latter in the making of great profit becomes quite secondary. When this stage is reached, the general stability and reputation of the institution are more considered by the management than the maximum of profit for the shareholders. The shareholders must be satisfied by conventionally adequate dividends; but once this is secured, the direct interest of the management often consists in avoiding criticism from the public and from the customers of the concern. This is particularly the case if their great size or semi-monopolistic position renders them conspicuous in the public eye and vulnerable to public attack.

Criticisms of the Doctrine

Economists have severely criticized the doctrine of socially responsible management because of its incompatibility with the price system. In the price system, rational calculation is carried on by sellers in order to maximize profits and by buyers to maximize consumption satisfaction. The market in which buyers and sellers come together is the control mechanism. There is no need for a central agency for planning and coordinating economic activity. All that is required for a price system is some standard upon which businessmen can base calculations of profit possibilities. Each seller makes decisions about which type of good to produce, the quality of the good, and the price to charge. Since there are many sellers all competing for the custom of the same buyers, competition among them controls their actions. Those who produce the goods most in demand and at prices consumers are willing to pay receive the highest profits.

The business enterprise must pursue the single goal of profit for the price system to work at maximum efficiency. It is the competitive interaction among enterprises in the market which activates the control mechanism in the price system. If businessmen take into account other goals besides profit, the price system loses much of its control over them. They become autonomous and no longer have an objective guideline for rational calculation. This interferes with the corporation's primary social function as the economizing unit in democratic capitalism. It performs the essential social task of allocating scarce resources in such a way as to bring about the greatest total economic satisfaction of the members of society. To the extent that it takes responsibility for accomplishing other broad social goals, the economizing process is interfered with and total economic satisfaction is reduced. Therefore, economists argue that the corporation should specialize in the production of goods and services and leave other social functions to the family, church, school, and government.

The concept of the conscience of the corporation has been particularly unacceptable to economists. Ben W. Lewis said,

> Certainly, if those who direct our corporate concentrates are to be free from regulation either by competition or government, I can only hope that they will be conscientious, responsible, and kindly men. . . . But, I shall be uneasy and a little ashamed . . . to be living my economic life within the limits set by the gracious bounty of the precious few. If we are to have rulers, let them be men of good will; but above all, let us join in choosing our rulers—and in ruling them.[6]

Carl Kaysen questioned the wisdom of displacing the invisible hand of the competitive market by the increasingly visible hand of powerful corporate management. This is irresponsible power, answerable only to itself, he charged. No matter how conscientious management is in balancing the interests of economic groups affected by the corporation, "it is ultimately its own conception of these interests and their desirable relations that rules."[7]

Much the same position has been taken by lawyers. Dean Rostow of the Yale Law School has said that a firmly stated and widely accepted rule that the social duty of managers is to serve the best interests of stockholders will offer a better guide to corporate practice than any of the current formulations of management's responsibility to society.[8] Wilber G. Katz, of the University of Chicago Law School, has misgivings about the doctrine of social responsibility because reliance on it may pave the way for destroying or weakening the institutions on which the traditional responsibility for economic performance rests.[9] The fundamental criticism of the doctrine from the legal point of view is the absence of control over managers. Berle believes that managers can be effectively controlled by "inchoate law," by which he means "rules of conduct whose disregard entails consequences almost as foreseeable as does violation of specific statutes such as the antitrust laws."[10] But lawyers believe in the "rule of law" and they want something more tangible to limit the wide scope of managerial discretion.

Political scientists criticize the doctrine because of the free rein it gives management. They mistrust any check on power other than power itself. Earl Latham has pointed out that power does not check power automatically and without human hands. "If the . . . power of the corporation is to be curbed and controlled, the checks will have to be built into the structure of corporate enterprise, and not just merely laid on from without, nor entrusted to the subjective bias of the hierarchs within."[11] In the same vein, Michael Reagan said that for us to "leave to the consciences of business managers the fate of all groups and interests touched by their decisions is to say that we will hand over to them power to affect all of our lives."[12]

Theodore Levitt has criticized the doctrine on broad social grounds. He says, "The business of business is profits. . . . In the end business has only two responsibilities—to obey the every-day face-to-face civility (honesty, good faith, and so on) and to seek material gain." He foresees the new orthodoxy leading to "a new feudalism," with the corporation investing itself "with all-embracing duties, obligations, and finally powers—ministering to the whole man and molding him and society in the image of the corporation's narrow ambitions and its essentially unsocial needs."[13]

Differences in Viewpoints of Supporters and Critics

The critics of the doctrine of socially responsible management view it from the historical perspective of Western man's struggle for individual freedom. The individual is the highest good in their value system. He is viewed as a reasoning being who is primarily motivated by a desire to maximize his individual welfare. Competitive markets are used to spur businessmen to greater efficiency and to dispense a stern but equitable justice to investors, workers, and resource owners; and reliance is placed on regulated self-interest to maintain social order. There is no elite which runs the capitalistic system because one is not needed. The invisible hand of the market assures attainment of social goals and group welfare. Organizations which concentrate power, particularly economic and political organizations, are viewed with suspicion. As Clark Kerr said, "This is the open society to which the western world has been dedicated for a century and a half. It is a society of accommodated conflict rather than universal collaboration."[14]

Underlying the criticisms of the doctrine is a strong ideological commitment to the market system. In addition to its economic function of directing resources into their most efficient use and maintaining a check on production costs, the market performs the ethical function of protecting and fostering the freedom of the individual and the political function of minimizing private power and protecting the rights of minority groups. The relationships between the economic, ethical, and political functions of the market system are expressed by Milton Friedman in the following five propositions:[15]

1 The fundamental question in a free society is: What is the best relationship between people?
2 The best relationship is that which maximizes freedom.
3 Maximum freedom requires the elimination of power or its dispersal.
4 The market disperses economic power most effectively and results in the greatest degree of individual economic freedom.
5 Without economic freedom there can be no political freedom.

The social thinkers whose writings implicitly support the doctrine of socially responsible management do not have the unanimity of the critics on matters of ideology and theory. Mayo's theoretical orientation is psychological, and his views are not based on any particular political or economic ideology. His starting point is the analysis of conditions necessary for individual mental health. From it he derives the idea that the manager's responsibility to society is to prevent social disorganization by introducing human relations into industry. Drucker, on the other hand, espouses the position of the philosophical conservative. His view of the good society is essentially that of Plato modified to fit the conditions of industrialism. Berle's views are those of an ideological determinist. He attempts to link the concept of Christian love to the conditions of economic growth. Keynes's ideological position is that of a reform liberal. He believes in individual freedom as strongly as Friedman. But he does not place all his trust in the market system, and he thinks large corporations administered by socially responsible managers are necessary to protect individual freedom in industrial society. The unifying theme in these four approaches is the idea that management must become a socially responsible elite in order to help overcome the serious structural and functional problems which threaten the collapse of Western civilization.

Evolution of the Doctrine

Some of the differences between supporters and critics are due, no doubt, to the fact that there have been six phases in the evolution of the doctrine of social responsibility:

1 *The principle of trusteeship of wealth in the 1890s:* The businessman is seen as a private individual who holds his wealth in trust for the nation.
2 *"Enlightened absolutism" at the turn of the century:* The all-powerful corporation begins to recognize its stake in the well-being of the workers.
3 *Corporate public relations before World War I:* Giant corporations attempt to win approval of the general public.
4 *The service concept of business in the 1920s:* Businessmen see mass production as the major contribution of business to society.

5 *The "sell free enterprise" campaign of the 1940s:* The business community attempts to quell criticisms of business originating in the Great Depression by educating the public about capitalism.

6 *The social responsibility doctrine full-blown since World War II:* Emergence of the idea of the corporate conscience.

The American dream of free land, economic freedom, and equal opportunity for all, which had been the guiding vision of millions of immigrants from Europe in the 1870s and 1880s, did not fit easily into the industrial reality of the 1890s. Class consciousness, which previously was not part of the American landscape, developed as the social and economic gap between employer and employee widened. The progressive movement emerged as a protest against big business and the decline of economic equality. The large fortunes the captains of industry had accumulated were widely criticized. There were signs that unless these fortunes could be justified in a way that would allay public criticism, they would be controlled through regulation of business. Business leaders recognized the threat. William J. Ghent, a severe critic of American business of the day, noted a greater self-consciousness of authority and responsibility among the industrial magnates as their power grew. He remarked on the tendency for the captains of industry to develop the paternalistic attitude of feudal lords, and he anticipated that eventually this trend would be checked by "a sense of the latent sense of democracy" and "a growing sense of ethics."[16]

The "seignorial" attitude of business leaders became formalized into the principle of trusteeship of wealth. This, of course, was not a new idea. Throughout history men have justified having more than their fellows on the ground that they are the chosen instruments of God to hold wealth in trust for the welfare of all. It is really not their own wealth, they argue, although they may benefit from it temporarily while it is in their keeping; they are merely stewards of what God has given. Thus Rockefeller in endowing the University of Chicago said, "The good Lord gave me my money, and how could I withhold it from the University of Chicago?"[17] Andrew Carnegie was the most articulate spokesman for the principle of trusteeship of wealth. The gospel of wealth which he preached proposed that surplus wealth be devoted to "the reconciliation of the rich and the poor—a reign of harmony" among men of all classes.[18]

The principle of the trusteeship of wealth was significant on two counts for the evolution of the doctrine of social responsibility. First, it was the earliest indication that the leading businessmen recognized the need to justify their wealth and power to society. As Ghent said, "The principle of the 'trusteeship of great wealth' has won a number of adherents. . . . A duty to society has been apprehended, and these are its first fruits. It is a duty, true enough, which is but dimly seen and imperfectly fulfilled."[19] Second, the justification was put in individual terms. Philanthropic activities of wealthy individuals were the means of fulfilling the businessman's duty to society rather than expressions of ethical concern for how the affairs of business enterprises were conducted. The focus was on what the captains of industry did with their millions after they had made them. They considered their actions in accumulating wealth to be another matter, private and beyond social criticism and control.

Corporations began to become directly involved in the welfare of their employees at the turn of the century. The railroads established a policy of financial support for the YMCA, and corporate contributions to charity began to occur in other industries. Management began to take an interest in safety and sanitary conditions in factories, and programs of payments were set up for accidents, retirement, and death. Management recognized the company's stake in the well-being of the workers, but often the objective of welfare activities was more ambitious. The Colorado Fuel and Iron Company, for example, announced that it was "the purpose of this corporation to solve the social problem."[20] Be it noted, however, that the "social problem" tended to be defined from the standpoint of the employer, with little regard for the needs and attitudes of others. Morrel Heald has termed these experiments in social and individual welfare "enlightened absolutism," calling attention to the fact that the corporation was still all-powerful but that it was beginning to recognize its obligations to those most directly affected by its operations.[21]

The corporation's obligation to society as a whole, in addition to the industrial workers, came into consideration in the pre-World War I years. The rapid growth and great size of some industrial firms created special problems and led management to seek a broad base of public support. The Bell System became a pioneer in corporate public relations because by combining a nationwide network of telephone facilities it had become a public utility. Its management, under the leadership of Theodore N. Vail, foresaw the inevitability of government regulation and welcomed rather than fought it. The Bell System concentrated on efficient and economical service, and attempted in every way possible to demonstrate management's conviction that, "We feel our obligation to the general public as strongly as to our investing public, or to our own personal interests."[22] The United States Steel Company and the Standard Oil Company also became public relations–conscious during this period. Elbert H. Gary, chairman of U.S. Steel, sensed the quasi-public nature of his company. Rockefeller and his associates became sensitive to the public criticism of Standard's hard-driving tactics and recognized that to a large segment of the public, economic performance alone was not the measure of its obligation to society.

Heald attributes the rise of the concept of social accountability of business enterprise in the first part of the twentieth century to three causes.

> the emergence of an economic order based increasingly upon large-scale enterprise with interests which affected an ever-widening circle of citizens. Secondly, popular reaction to this change and the resulting activities of state and national governments led business leaders to see their ultimate dependence upon a favorable social climate and the need for more than economic performance alone in order to maintain that climate.

The third cause was the response of the nation to World War I. The war called for self-sacrifice, a mobilization of the entire economy, and massive, organized welfare programs in Europe after the armistice. Business accepted its share of responsibility in the war effort and contributed funds and leadership. The practice of corporate giving for community welfare programs was firmly established. Corporations developed a sense of social responsibility which declined but did not disappear entirely after the war.[23]

In the peaceful and prosperous 1920s, there was a growing awareness by business leaders of the broader implications of mass production. During this decade business was no longer defensive. It was seldom subjected to the acrimonious criticism it had experienced in the age of the muckrakers. Management had the opportunity to take to the offense in order to maintain the prestige and leadership regained during the war years. It did so by preaching the message of the service performed by business in the public interest. It defined "service" in accordance with its own view of the social obligations of business, and the emphasis was on the increase in production and productivity. Mass production, it was argued, is the major contribution of business to individual and social welfare.

Edward A. Filene, a leading spokesman for business, said, "It is the discovery that it pays to give service, and that it pays best to give the greatest possible service to the greatest possible number, which is now not only revolutionizing business but revolutionizing the whole world in which we live." Service, according to Filene, was not only the means to profit under mass production; it offered hope for "the liberation of the masses."[24]

The Great Depression brought renewed attacks on business. Rightly or wrongly business, and particularly big business, was blamed for the breakdown of the economy. The realignment of political power among economic interest groups under the New Deal weakened the position of business and strengthened that of labor and agriculture and other potential critics of business. World War II brought an end to the Depression and gave business the opportunity to demonstrate once again its importance to the nation in time of war. In the postwar period the business community has attempted to maintain its relative position and wherever possible advance it through public relations campaigns. During the late 1940s and early 1950s, there was a particularly intensive effort to improve the climate for business. According to William Whyte, "Businessmen appeared . . . gripped with a single idea . . . We must *sell* Free Enterprise."[25] Whyte estimates 100 million dollars a year was spent on reselling the virtues of the American free enterprise system to the American people (with visual aids ranging from a General Motors full length Hollywood movie on the profit system to the free enterprise comic books of Procter and Gamble). The free enterprise sales campaign was a failure. Business leaders found that they were talking to themselves; the American people simply were not listening because they did not believe that old ideology could solve new and vexing problems.

Throughout this century the idea has been growing that the corporation has a social obligation that goes beyond producing goods and services and that management is responsible ultimately to society rather than investors. As early as 1908, George Perkins, a director of U.S. Steel and International Harvester, argued that, "The larger the corporation becomes, the greater becomes its responsibilities to the entire community." He believed that big-business corporations must be "semi-public servants, serving the public, with ownership widespread among the public, and with labor so fairly and equitably treated that it will look upon its corporation as its friend. . . ."[26] The same line was taken by Prof. Merrick Dodd, Jr., in a 1932 *Harvard Law Review* article in which he argued that managers should be recognized as legally free from the obligation to maximize profits in the stockholders' behalf. He believed that managers ought to concentrate on conducting the affairs of the corporation in a socially responsible manner because they are trustees of corporate wealth and power for society as a whole, not merely for the stockholders.[27] In *The Modern Corporation and Private Property,* published in 1932, Berle and Means stated that if the corporate system is to survive, it is almost essential "that the 'control' of the great corporations should develop into a purely neutral technocracy, balancing a variety of claims by various groups in the community and assigning to each a portion of the income stream on the basis of public policy rather than private cupidity."[28]

Thus the doctrine of social responsibility is a new version of the trustee-ship principle: It is the corporation with all its power that is given by society to management as a public trust rather than the wealth put into the hands of individuals by God. This idea has been widely disseminated by Adolf Berle in his book *The 20th Century Capitalist Revolution,* in which he puts forth the idea that corporations have a conscience. Berle takes the position that economic power is absolute, and therefore managers must exercise their power without every decision being reviewed by court, investigating commission, or regulatory authority. If this were not so, such reviewing bodies would be substituting their business judgment for that of management. Managers have no choice but to use the power placed in their hands if they are not to lose it by default to someone else; probably the state. But absolute power always calls forth a counter-vailing force to check it. Berle believes that the only real control which guides or limits the economic and social action of managers is their real, though undefined and tacit, philosophy. He concludes that "the corpora-tion, almost against its will, has been compelled to assume in appreciable part the role of conscience-carrier of the twentieth-century American so-ciety." It has done this through day-to-day decisions, "without intent to dominate and without clearly defined doctrine."[29]

Interpretations of Social Responsibility

Another reason for the differences between supporters and critics of socially responsible management is that the concept can be interpreted in five different ways:

1 *Social responsibility as covert profit maximization:* The manager is still a profit maximizer but he recognizes that changes in the social and political environment of business require him to adopt the posture of social responsibility.

2 *Social responsibility as heeding the public consensus:* If the manager does anything considered wrong or improper by the public, he is punished.

3 *Social responsibility as the balancing of the various interests affected by the corporation:* The manager looks upon himself as an impartial arbiter.

4 *Social responsibility as business statesmanship:* The manager utilizes the resources of the corporation to bring about a better world.

5 *Social responsibility as fulfillment of the manager role:* The manager behaves in a socially responsible way by living up to his role expectations.

The view that social responsibility is covert profit maximization has the appearance of bridging the gap between the profit ethic and the ethic of social responsibility. Writers who take this position put the analysis into the long-run time dimension. They point out that the corporation is a creature of the state and in a democracy society controls the state. Therefore, if the members of society become displeased with the corporation, they can destroy it and put another form of economic organization in its place. Over the long run, therefore, the corporation must meet the demands of society if it is to survive. Managers must be alert to social trends and conduct the affairs of the corporation in accordance with them. If society demands more socially responsible behavior from corporations, managers will behave in the required way. But the underlying goal still remains profit maximization. Managers are only willing to behave in socially responsible ways that reduce short-run profits because they must for the corporation to survive. By surviving they "optimize"—earn the largest possible profit in the long run.

This interpretation of social responsibility would be valid only if Adam Smith's conception of man as an inherently selfish being were correct. Smith based his economic ideas on the egoistic theory of motivation which had been formulated earlier by Thomas Hobbes and Jeremy Bentham. This theory has been accepted by most economists from Adam Smith's time until the present, but it has been rejected by psychologists and philosophers. The idea of self-interest, in its broadest sense, means *anything* the self happens to be identified with. In Adam Smith's day the members of the rising business class were interested in making money. It was an understandable error, therefore, to think of pecuniary acquisitiveness as an inherent characteristic of human nature. But the self can be identified with many other things besides accumulation of wealth (e.g., helping the underprivileged, pursuit of a fascinating hobby, enjoyment of aesthetic experiences). All conduct is not necessarily in behalf of the acquisitive kind of self. "Thus, psychological egoism must be either trivial or false: in the use in which it has significance it is false; in the use in which it is true it is trivial."[30] One could just as well use the self-interest theory of motivation to argue that the modern manager identifies his self with the values, goals, and needs of society and therefore behaves in a socially responsible manner.

Adolf Berle has defined social responsibility as the manager's responsiveness to the public consensus. This is a step removed from the covert profit-maximization view because it assumes no particular theory of human motivation and it does imply variation in management goals and behavior over time. Presumably profit will be a more important social goal at one time than at another. When it is an important social goal, managers will pursue it because if they do not, they will run afoul of the public consensus and sanctions will be invoked. The difficulty with this view is that it is entirely negative. Managers learn *what not to do* by public reaction, but the concept of public consensus does not provide any positive guidelines for them to follow. Furthermore, there is likely to be a lag between the time managers take an antisocial step and the time public consensus can be mobilized into public opinon so that managers realize their error and try to correct it.

The balancer-of-interests approach appeals very much to many socially oriented top managers. They see themselves as occupying a strategic position in the center of the network of corporate relations. They mediate between the demands of workers, unions, customers, stockholders, suppliers, distributors, the community, and government. This view of social responsibility is accurate *as far as it goes*. It does describe the manager's position. But it does not tell us anything about the source of the manager's ideas about how the various interests should be balanced. How, for example, does a manager decide whether a saving effected by an innovation in production technique should be passed on to the customer in the form of a better product or a lower price, to workers as a wage increase, or to stockholders?

The view that socially responsible managers are business statesmen has an answer to this question: The manager simply makes the decision that he thinks is best for the country as a whole. If he believes that inflation is our number one economic problem, he cuts the price of the product; if inadequate demand is the problem, he will raise the workers' wages; if capital is needed for automation, the savings will be plowed back into the firm and will enhance the stockholders' equity. The difficulty with this approach, however, is that it places too great a burden on the manager. He must be a philosopher, a seer, an economist, and a social thinker if he is to perform effectively as a business statesman. But where can he get the experience and education necessary to be all of these things? Furthermore, by temperament most managers are activity oriented and unused to philosophical speculation.

The most satisfactory interpretation of social responsibility for analytical purposes is that of the manager fulfilling the expectations of his social role. From the sociological viewpoint, society is a social system made up of different statuses (e.g., farmer, manager, husband, son). Individuals occupy various statuses; a man may be a manager, Rotarian, Republican, Methodist, and so on. Associated with each status is a role, the ways of behaving expected of the occupant of the status. When a status occupant behaves as he is expected to, he is rewarded; when he does not, he is punished. He goes through a period of socialization to learn how to behave in accordance with his role. From this viewpoint all behavior is socially responsible in the sense that it conforms to generally accepted norms. Therefore, the manager is by definition socially responsible as long as he does not deviate significantly from his role expectations. This means that if society wants the manager to maximize profits and so delineates his social role, the socially responsible thing to do is to maximize profits. That is what happened in the Age of Enterprise. But today profit maximization is no longer the sole expectation of the manager role. It is expected that the manager will conduct the affairs of the corporation in such a way as to accomplish a balance among a wide range of objectives.

This approach overcomes the limitations of the other four. It is based on the idea that man is a social animal rather than an economic man. He basically wants to do what is considered right by society. Even if he is selfish and hard-driving, he will attempt to attain his goals in socially prescribed ways (unless he is a criminal deviate). Therefore, this interpretation does not rely on the egoistic theory of motivation. Since managers are socialized in order to perform their roles effectively, they have some idea of what is expected of them, and they try to do what is right and not merely avoid doing what is wrong. The status of the manager corresponds to the position he has in the balancer-of-interests interpretation. The source of his ideas of how to balance the interests is his role. Since the role is limited to certain types of behavior and defined in fairly concrete terms, the manager need not be a business statesman.

When we talk about *socially responsible managers,* what we are really doing is calling attention to a particular type of emphasis in the expectations of the manager role. We are not indicating a radical new relationship between the businessman and society. In the Age of Enterprise, the entrepreneur aggressively pursued profit for its own sake. It is a mistake, however, to interpret this self-seeking activity as antisocial. On the contrary, it was precisely what society required at the time for the capital accumulation that was needed to attain a high rate of economic growth. Entrepreneurs were *allowed* to behave in an essentially selfish way because such behavior was well suited to the industrialization of the economy that was the required means to achieving a higher standard of living for all the members of society.

Now that the most arduous part of the task of building an industrial economy has been completed, a new type of behavior is coming to be expected of business leaders. The vast power that society has placed in their hands must now be used to achieve a different set of objectives than those envisaged by the captains of industry. Since these objectives are more explicitly social in character than profit making appears to be, it is not surprising that many observers conclude that the socially responsible manager is now trying to serve social ends, whereas his nineteenth-century predecessors did not. But the entrepreneur and manager roles cannot be distinguished on the basis of which one is more socially oriented, because they both are instrumental means to social ends. The basic difference between them is in the nature of the ends which they serve. The role of the modern manager cannot be the same as that of the nineteenth-century entrepreneur because of the vast changes that have occurred in the social systems of the economy and society.

Problems of the Doctrine

The differences in viewpoint of the critics and supporters of the doctrine of social responsibility can be analyzed in terms of four basic problems:

1 *Status of the corporation and manager:* What are their positions in American society?
2 *Functions of the corporation and manager:* Which, if any, functions other than the economic task of producing goods and services should they perform?
3 *Power of the corporation and manager:* On what grounds can the economic and political power of the corporation and manager be justified?
4 *Control of the corporation and manager:* How can society control the corporation and manager?

The problem of status. Before the corporate and managerial revolutions, the social statuses of the corporation and manager were clear-cut. The corporation was a private organization pursuing the single goal of profit. It was well regarded because it exemplified the strong materialistic element in the American value system. The captains of industry also were looked up to. They made fortunes building new industries and were the epitome of the free American in the new industrial milieu. The statuses of the corporation and the businessman were unambiguous in terms of their relations with other entities in society. These relations were based entirely on the exchange process in the market. The corporation bought and hired inputs in resource, labor, and money markets, and it produced outputs for sale in goods and service markets. Its specialized economic function limited the relations it had with other social entities.

The corporate revolution brought about significant changes in the status of the corporation. Its social standing became ambivalent. On the one hand, people admired the strength and success of the large corporation; but on the other, they were fearful and suspicious of it because of its concentrated power. Its relation to other social structures became ambiguous. As the large corporation became a general social institution rather than a specialist economic organization, these relations became more important, complicated, and harder to trace and understand. The clear line of demarcation between the private and public sectors of social and economic activity became blurred. It is not clear today whether the corporation has the status of the key coordinating institution in society (as

Drucker would like) or still maintains its specialized economic status, only interpreted somewhat more broadly than in the past. The doctrine of socially responsible management tells us nothing on this score.

The same kind of ambiguity surrounds the status of the manager. The separation of ownership and control has given management an autonomy that is difficult to fit into the concept of private property. Managers no longer seem compelled to be responsible to stockholders. The doctrine of socially responsible management implies that somehow managers are accountable to society at large. But what is the nature of this relationship? How can one occupational group which holds power based neither on property ownership nor political election be related to all the groups in society subject to its power? A new theory of big business must develop before these questions can be answered.

The problem of function. Closely related to the problem of status is that of function. In addition to expanding greatly in size in recent years, the corporation has expanded functionally. It no longer is just a producer of goods and services. It now performs a number of political, welfare, social, and cultural functions as well as its primary economic function. In short, the big-business corporation has become a multipurpose social institution.

Since the end of World War II, corporations have tended to perform noneconomic functions to a greater extent than ever before. They have operated during most of this period at a fairly high level of capacity utilization, and on the whole they have had a favorable profit experience. They have been able to perform their primary economic function satisfactorily with respect to the national interest and their own welfare. At the same time, they have grown and become stronger financially, so that their capacity to perform social functions has expanded. Furthermore, there has been an increasing demand by the public that corporations be more socially responsible and behave in ways that are considered beneficial to the community.

As we have seen, economists are opposed to noneconomic functions of the corporation because they interfere with the corporation's traditional function of serving as society's chief economizing agent in the allocation of scarce resources. Political scientists have misgivings about corporate functions which are public in nature and traditionally have been the prerogatives of the state. They question whether the tendency of the corporation to take on political functions is in keeping with the pluralistic tradition of American social structure and political processes. Cultural objections to the trend are based on a dislike of the tendency for corporate values and goals to become the common denominator by which values and goals in all walks of life are judged. Those who oppose noneconomic corporate functions on social grounds fear that this development may be carried so far that the open society will be destroyed and we will enter a new age of corporate feudalism.

Managers who subscribe to the doctrine of socially responsible management have a congenial attitude toward secondary noneconomic functions of the corporation. The doctrine itself is vague, however, about which functions the corporation ought to perform. Should the socially responsible manager conduct the affairs of the corporation in such a way as to bring about a better world for us all? If so, there ought to be no limitations placed on the functions performed by the corporation. Few Americans would agree to such a broad interpretation of the manager's social mandate. But if there is anything to the doctrine of socially responsible management, the corporation should perform at least some noneconomic functions. But which ones, and upon what grounds of legitimacy?

The problem of power. The problems of status and function would not be significant if it were not for the growth in the size of the corporation and the great power which this growth has brought about. There are two aspects of the power problem: the concentration of corporate power and the legitimacy of management power.

The concentration of corporate power is primarily an economic problem. Many economists believe that the ideal economy is one composed of purely competitive markets in which many small firms are closely controlled by competition. According to this view, the market performs the essential social task of economizing by channeling resources into their most efficient use and maintaining a check on production costs. Clearly industries dominated by large corporations do not have the decentralization of economic power which is the prime requisite of the economists' model of pure competition. This structural characteristic is the basis of most of the criticisms made by economists of big business. These criticisms were put into the following five categories by J. D. Glover after he made a careful survey of the economics literature attacking the large corporation:[31]

1 *Big business cannot be managed efficiently:* Administration is essentially authoritarian, and it becomes despotic in the very large organization. Perhaps this is necessary to hold the large corporation together so that it can function as a coherent whole, but despotism does not lead to good decisions and an efficient organization.

2 *Big business does not owe its growth to efficiency:* The impetus behind the rise of big business was the desire for monopoly power, not economic efficiency. The promoters who put together huge industrial combinations did so not to reduce costs of production, but to take advantage of the opportunity to profit at the expense of investors.

3 *Statistics show that big business is not efficient:* To the extent that big business makes a poor statistical showing, that is due to its inefficiency. To the extent that it makes a good showing, that is due to monopoly economic power.

4 *The economies of big business are not net for society:* If a large corporation is profitable, it is because (a) it is able to exact monopoly gains, and/or (b) it is able to lower its own costs in a way that is of no advantage to society at large since it is simply a matter of shifting costs on to other elements in the economy.

5 *Big business holds back invention:* The large corporation has a monopoly position and therefore has little to fear from competition. Consequently the rate of technological progress is slower in big business than in smaller enterprises.

These criticisms clearly indicate the unwillingness of economists to accept the good intentions of responsible managers in place of the rigors of market competition. The existence of great corporate power is a precondition for the doctrine of socially responsible management. Without such concentrated power, it would not matter whether managers were socially responsible or not. Presumably whatever their intentions, they would be constrained by market forces to behave in ways which in the final analysis would turn out to be best for society.

The problem of the legitimacy of management power is basically a political one. The large corporation frequently is criticized as being an undemocratic institution. By democracy we generally mean a political system in which those persons who are in positions of authority receive their power from the people over whom it is exercised and use the power in conformity with the wishes of the majority. Therefore, for power to be consistent with democratic principles, it must (1) be legitimate (i.e., derived with the consent of the governed), and (2) be exercised responsibly (i.e., in accordance with the will of the majority). Whether or not an organization is democratic depends on whether its leaders acquire their power legitimately and whether the power can be taken away from them if it is exercised irresponsibly.

As we have seen, a few thousand top managers actively control the destinies of big business in America. But who selected these men, and to whom are they responsible? The answer to the first question is easy: They selected themselves. The management groups of large corporations are self-perpetuating oligarchies. One of the major tasks of aging top executives is to select and groom their successors. There is no generally accepted answer to the question of management responsibility, however, and it constitutes the problem of the legitimacy of management power. Those with a legal orientation argue that corporate managers must be responsible to the stockholders. They contend that if the link between the owners and managers is ever entirely dissolved, management will lose the legal basis for its existence. What real claim will managers have to their positions, they ask, if they do not own the company or represent the owners' interests? The implication of this line of reasoning is clear: To the extent that management is not directly responsible to the stockholders, its powers are not legitimate and big business is undemocratic.

The problem of control. According to classical economic theory, three forces control the activities of business firms: competition, the profit motive, and consumer sovereignty. As we have seen, social control of the corporation by competition has declined since the rise of big business and the profit motive has become less significant since it no longer provides managers with an unequivocal rule of action.

According to the doctrine of consumer sovereignty, consumers place a constraint on the activities of firms through the purchase choices they make. If they are to survive, firms must produce the kinds of goods and services which satisfy customers. But in an economy in which many billions of dollars are spent annually on advertising, style change, and sales promotion, the producer is not completely at the mercy of his customers. There is a measure of producer sovereignty too. It is not clear whether large corporations produce the goods which the consumers want to consume or if consumers consume the goods which the corporations want to produce.

If competition, the profit motive, and consumer sovereignty do not control big business, what does? Economists are uneasy about the large corporation because it seems to be running without any discernible controls. This is more of a basis for their criticism of big business than the belief that large corporations actually perform poorly in the public interest.

The doctrine of socially responsible management implies that the economists' view of the corporation as the locus of social control of economic activity is misleadingly anthropomorphic. The phrase "social control of the corporation" suggests that the corporation is a living entity which can control its own behavior in response to external stimuli. This, of course, is untrue. Social control is a process by which behavior is influenced to conform to some set of norms. For it to be effective, it must act on human beings because only they can consciously determine patterns of behavior. Organizations such as corporations are abstractions—communication networks tying together social systems of men performing interrelated roles with the aid of various kinds of capital. A corporation is not a person except in a fictional legal sense. It cannot do the things necessary to control its own behavior: think, evaluate, make decisions, and implement policies. Only human beings can do these things. Therefore, society cannot control the corporation directly; it must do so indirectly through the manager, the controller of the corporation. It must influence him to make the decisions that are in accordance with social needs.

Berle's idea about how society controls managers through social consensus has been severely criticized. Economists question the wisdom of displacing the invisible hand of the competitive market with the heavy hand of powerful corporate management. Edward S. Mason, former president of the American Economic Association, has summed up these criticisms and called upon the academic proponents of the doctrine of socially responsible management to produce a "managerial apologetic"—an up-to-date, generally acceptable explanation of how society controls corporations through managers.[32] Thus far no such explanation has appeared.

NOTES

1   Elton Mayo, *The Human Problems of an Industrial Civilization* (New York: The Macmillan Company, 1933), p. 188.
2   *Ibid.,* p. 149.

3   Peter F. Drucker, *The End of Economic Man* (New York: The John Day Company, Inc., 1939); *Concept of the Corporation* (New York: The John Day Company, Inc., 1946); *The New Society* (New York: Harper & Row, Publishers, Incorporated, 1950).

4   Adolf A. Berle, Jr., *The American Economic Republic* (New York: Harcourt, Brace & World, Inc., 1963).

5   John Maynard Keynes, "The End of Laissez-faire" (1926), reprinted in *Essays in Persuasion* (New York: W. W. Norton & Company, Inc., 1963), pp. 314–315.

6   Ben W. Lewis, "Economics by Admonition," *American Economic Review, Papers and Proceedings,* vol. 49, no. 2 (May, 1959), p. 395.

7   Carl Kaysen, "The Corporation: How Much Power? What Scope?" in Edward S. Mason (ed.), *The Corporation in Modern Society* (Cambridge, Mass.: Harvard University Press, 1959), p. 99.

8   Eugene V. Rostow, *Planning for Freedom: The Public Law of American Capitalism* (New Haven, Conn.: Yale University Press, 1959).

9   Wilber G. Katz, "Responsibility and the Modern Corporation," *Journal of Law and Economics,* vol. 3 (October, 1960), pp. 75–85.

10   Adolf A. Berle, Jr., *Power without Property* (New York: Harcourt, Brace & World, Inc., 1959).

11   Earl Latham, "The Body Politic of the Corporation," in Mason, *op. cit.,* p. 228.

12   Michael D. Reagan, *The Managed Economy* (Fair Lawn, N.J.: Oxford University Press, 1963), p. 125.

13   Theodore Levitt, "The Dangers of Social Responsibility," *Harvard Business Review,* vol. 36, no. 5 (September–October, 1959), pp. 41–50.

14   Clark Kerr, *Labor and Management in Industrial Society* (Garden City, N.Y.: Anchor Books, Doubleday & Company, Inc., 1964), pp. 77–78.

15   Milton Friedman, *Capitalism and Freedom* (Chicago: The University of Chicago Press, 1962).

16   William J. Ghent, *Our Benevolent Feudalism* (New York: The Macmillan Company, 1902), pp. 9–47.

17   Quoted in Ralph Henry Gabriel, *The Course of American Democratic Thought* (New York: The Ronald Press Company, 1940), p. 149.

18   Andrew Carnegie, *The Gospel of Wealth* (Garden City, N.Y.: Doubleday & Company, Inc., 1933), p. 11.

19   Ghent, *op. cit.,* pp. 182ff., passim.

20   *Ibid.,* p. 61.

21 Morrel Heald, "Management's Responsibility to Society: The Growth of an Idea," *The Business History Review,* vol. 31, no. 4 (Winter, 1957), p. 377.

22 From the 1913 *Annual Report* of the Bell System.

23 Heald, *op. cit.,* p. 379.

24 Edward A. Filene, "A Simple Code of Business Ethics," *Annals of the American Academy of Political and Social Sciences,* vol. 101 (May, 1922), pp. 223–228.

25 William H. Whyte, Jr., and the editors of *Fortune, Is Anybody Listening?* (New York: Simon and Schuster, Inc., 1952), pp. 4–6.

26 George W. Perkins, *The Modern Corporation* (New York: Columbia University Press, 1908), quoted in Heald, *op cit.,* pp. 378–379.

27 Merrick Dodd, Jr., "For Whom Are Corporate Managers Trustees?" *Harvard Law Review,* vol. 45 (1932), pp. 1145–1157.

28 Adolf A. Berle, Jr., and Gardiner C. Means, *The Modern Corporation and Private Property* (New York: The Macmillan Company, 1932), p. 356.

29 Adolf A. Berle, Jr., *The 20th Century Capitalist Revolution* (New York: Harcourt, Brace & World, Inc., 1954), p. 182.

30 Harry K. Girvetz, *The Evolution of Liberalism* (New York: Collier Books, Crowell-Collier Publishing Co., 1963), p. 159.

31 J. D. Glover, *The Attack on Big Business* (Boston: Harvard Graduate School of Business Administration, Division of Research, 1954), part 1. (Italics supplied.)

32 Edward S. Mason, "The Apologetics of 'Managerialism,'" *Journal of Business,* vol. 31, no. 1 (January, 1958), pp. 1–11.

5
Social
Responsibility
and Economic
Ideology

In earlier chapters the view was put forth that business ethics is at a turning point because the present moral crisis in management is in the process of being resolved. It was pointed out that a business ethic, to be acceptable to society, must be compatible with prevailing economic ideology and theory. This chapter analyzes the relation between the concept of social responsibility and economic ideology, and the next one analyzes the relation between social responsibility and economic theory. We shall see that changes in economic ideology and theory are already underway which are likely to make the concept of social responsibility acceptable before long to the business community and general public and thus help bridge the gap between operational and ideological business ethics and resolve the moral crisis in management.

Liberalism as the Ideology of Capitalism

Some economists reject the possibility of reconciling big business and capitalism because the dispersion of economic power required for thoroughgoing price competition is not found in industries dominated by big business. They believe that if capitalism is to be saved, we must break up big business. Stigler has argued that we would have a more productive economy without big business because large corporations have not achieved economies of operation but have reduced the effectiveness of competition.[1] The evidence on production diseconomies of scale in big business is scanty and inconclusive, however. The best empirical study to date, that of Bain, concluded that there are substantial economies of scale that justify economic concentration in some industries but not in others.[2] It is likely, at least in the near future, that most Americans will continue to believe that big business contributes substantially to our economic abundance, and economists will not be able to come up with the hard facts necessary to change their minds.

A choice between big business and capitalism would involve a serious conflict in values for most Americans. On the one hand, we respond strongly to the argument that a free society should have a competitive economy. Many of the values we believe in most fervently, such as freedom, democracy, progress, and equality, are strongly associated with the concept of capitalism. But on the other hand, we believe big business is largely responsible for our high standard of living, and for that reason

The moral crisis in management

we do not want to give it up. We value it because of the de
of materialism in the American national character. We face a c
when the nonmaterial values associated with capitalism are pitted a ...ist
the material values associated with big business.

But is it necessary that America choose between big business and capitalism? Why cannot we have both? The argument that we must choose
between the two is based on the assumption that capitalism is a particular
type of economic system, one in which private property, the profit motive,
the market system, and *laissez faire* play vital roles. But is this necessarily
so? Do these institutions *define* capitalism or merely *describe* it at a particular stage of development?

The concept of capitalism was first analyzed by socialist theorists, particularly Karl Marx. They based their work largely on the writings of
Ricardo and other members of the British school of classical economics.
The classical economists did not conceive of capitalism as a particular
type of economic system. In keeping with the then popular theory of
unilinear evolution, they thought there was only one type of economy
and that capitalism represented its most advanced stage. Socialist writers,
of course, held different views. They believed that it would be possible
to develop a socialist economy that retained the best features of capitalism
and dispensed with what they considered to be its inhuman aspects and
inherent contradictions and weaknesses. Consequently they were extremely
critical of capitalism and stressed its political and ethical deficiencies.
Nonsocialist economists tended to avoid the term entirely, except in connection with the history of economic doctrines, because of their desire
to avoid value judgments which they considered outside the scope of
economics.

It is impossible to deal with the concept of capitalism in any depth,
however, without getting into the realm of values. The socialist critics
were on solid methodological ground in this respect, regardless of whether
one agrees with their arguments or point of view. Indeed, the entire
justification of capitalism must be found in values. This is particularly
true today when we are not so sure as we used to be that capitalism
is the most productive economic system. But what values can justify capitalism? To answer this question we must place capitalism in its historical
setting. Then we see that it developed in response to a strongly felt need
to reorganize social and political as well as economic arrangements.

Feudalism and mercantilism were opposite solutions to the problem of the proper relations between individuals and between the individual and the state. Feudalism solved the problem in a lawless age in which there was no state to protect the individual by organizing social, political, and economic life on a tightly knit local basis. The feudal emphasis on the responsibilities that the members of each social class owed to each other left little room for individual freedom to flower. Feudalism was followed by mercantilism, a system which tended to sacrifice the individual for the greater glory of the state. It in turn was followed by capitalism which, along with its political correlate democracy, arose to free the individual from arbitrary coercion by the state.

The values that capitalism is most strongly associated with stem from the social philosophy of liberalism. This philosophy arose to deal with the great social problem of political authority versus individual autonomy that resulted from the clash between the individualism of the Renaissance and the emergence of the nation-state in the sixteenth century.

Capitalism owed much of its vitality in the eighteenth and nineteenth centuries to the welding together of the individualistic values of liberalism and unabashed materialism. There was no conflict between the two types of values and goals. The individual bent on making his fortune did so in the belief that property and money were not only necessary for a comfortable life, but also the means to the noble end of moral freedom. The person who was financially independent could not be coerced by economic forces to behave in ways that went against his conscience. Thus capitalism was not only a set of economic institutions that described the workings of the economic system; it was also the manifestation in economic life of a philosophy that reflected the most powerful social and political drives of the age.

Capitalism, then, is most fundamentally an economic system organized to promote the values in the social philosophy of liberalism. As long as the economy is organized to promote these values and their related goals, the economic system is capitalistic regardless of the economic institutions employed. Economic institutions such as private property, the profit motive, the market system, and *laissez faire* are merely means to capitalistic ends, and they are expendable. A set of economic institutions that is most effective in achieving the desired results in one set of historical circumstances may be entirely inappropriate in another. All that can be said of any particular set of economic institutions is that they *describe* a particular stage of capitalism; they never *define* capitalism as a generic system. The definition of capitalism must always be related to the liberal values that it furthers.

Thus although capitalism promotes and protects liberal values, it is liberalism which gives capitalism its inner meaning. Another way of putting it is to say that liberalism is the ideology of capitalism. It provides a more or less unified system of ideas, values, norms, and beliefs which makes understandable to men the arrangements by which they make their livings in a capitalist system. The analysis of this section suggests that both capitalism and its ideology, liberalism, are dynamic rather than static. Changes in historical circumstances bring about changes in both the structure and functioning of capitalism and the meaning of liberalism.

From Market Capitalism to Controlled Capitalism

Werner Sombart, the German economic historian, analyzed the evolution of capitalism from the beginning of the Renaissance to the present. He thought the third and final stage of capitalist development, "late capitalism," began with World War I and is continuing today. In this period industrialization spreads throughout the world and the gap between industrial and agricultural countries closes. The purely capitalistic elements of the economy become weaker as the groups who were disadvantaged during the previous period of "full capitalism" organize and promote their interests politically. The business enterprise continues to grow larger. There is a decline in business risk and an increase in business planning based on systematic calculation. Speculation and intuition of the entrepreneur give way to careful budgeting of production, finances, and sales. The large-scale private business organization looks more like a public agency than a capitalist enterprise. The quest for profit declines as dividend rates become fixed, reinvestment of surplus is planned, risk taking becomes specialized, and reserves are created. Eventually there is a general decay of the capitalist spirit.[3]

Since the appearance of Sombart's theory in 1927, economists have analyzed the evolution of capitalism. It is now agreed that "pure" capitalism has evolved into a "mixed" economy. An explanation of this transformation that is becoming widely accepted is that the capitalistic system has been reformed from within by private and governmental action to remove specific defects. Influential non-Marxist interpretations of this tranformation are Karl Polanyi's theory of social protection and Bruno Seidel's theory of the taming of private capitalism.

Polanyi thinks that the market system is the cause of the major economic woes of the past two centuries and that it nearly succeeded in wrecking Western civilization. His analysis of capitalism focuses on how the market system brought about economic disadvantage to various groups by emphasizing the naturalistic and deemphasizing the humanistic approach to economic organization. He argues that the application of the laws of supply and demand to farming and industry created great evils for the farmer and landlord, the colonials in underdeveloped countries, the worker in modern industry, and the business firm itself. The principle of social protection developed to overcome these evils. Its aim was "the conservation of man and nature as well as productive organization," and its method was the use of "protective legislation, restrictive associations, and other instruments of intervention."[4]

Polanyi's concept of social protection is so broad that it covers all deviations from the idealized market system through collective action by interest groups or the state (e.g., monopoly, cartels, imperialism, social insurance, indirect subsidies to farmers, national liberation in colonies). As Arthur Schweitzer pointed out, Polanyi's defect theory of private capitalism is weakened by the lack of a specific market analysis which indicates how specific disadvantages arise in the process of pricing. His concept of social protection contains so many diverse elements that it is impossible to infer from it a theory of how interventions have reformed the market system.[5] Nonetheless Polanyi's general conclusions—that there has been a steady collectivization of economic life and that the market system has been undermined by intervention of government and various economic interest groups—cannot be gainsaid.

Seidel's analysis of evolving capitalism focuses on the nature of the relation between industrialism and capitalism. The Industrial Revolution added industrialism to capitalism, and a conflict has arisen between these two elements in the present economic system. The great dilemma of our time, according to Seidel, is caused by our ability to tame the capitalist features of the economy but our inability to control the industrial elements of the capitalist economy.

Industrialism, with its large-scale production units, mechanization and automation, and high level of specialization and social and economic interdependence, has penetrated deeply into all phases of human activity;

and it has created a new type of industrial man and industrial style of life.[6] On the other hand, capitalism, with its private property, free market mechanism, and cyclical fluctuations in employment, has increasingly become subjected to nonmarket controls. Modern technology is allowed to develop freely, but the market system is restricted and reformed. Interventions of three types occur: (1) the social-political interventions of trade unions, which are made possible by the spread of democracy and the increased political strength of labor; (2) organizational interventions of producers (e.g., cartels, price fixing, production quotas) to gain control over their markets; and (3) socioethical interventions of the state to achieve greater security and equality. These interventions tame capitalism and lead to a system made up of capitalistic and socialistic elements which, in effect, produce a dual economy.

The mixed system that is now found in every non-Communist Western nation is referred to by a variety of names. Most of them convey the idea that the economy is still basically capitalistic—since it remains a market economy in which fundamental allocation decisions are made by private firms—but that it is a modified form of capitalism because of the vastly enlarged role of government. They do this by adding an adjective to capitalism: people's capitalism, guided capitalism, welfare capitalism, controlled capitalism. The latter term will be used here because it has the connotation of a system in which private property and free enterprise exist but in which control is exercised by the state and various private agencies to prevent unemployment and to foster economic growth, security, and equality.

Andrew Shonfield, director of studies at the British Royal Institute of International Affairs, cites the following as outstanding institutional features of controlled capitalism:[7]

1 *The important role played by government.* This role varies from one country to another. In one the control of the banking system by the central bank may be decisive, in another large-scale use of public enterprise may be the means. In all western European countries public planning is an important means of government control of the economy.

2 *A preoccupation with social welfare.* Public funds are being devoted on a larger scale than ever before to support people who do not earn, primarily students and retired persons. Outlays for education

and pensions absorb an increasing percentage of national income in advanced capitalist countries.

3 *The violence of the market has been tamed.* Competition still exists but it is increasingly regulated and controlled. There is more long-range collaboration between business and government. Governmental planners encourage firms in the same industry to evolve common policies in order to improve the validity of predictions and thus make long-range planning more effective.

4 *Annual increase in per capita real income is taken for granted.* Acceleration of technological innovation will make this expectation a reality for a long time to come. But new forms of organization and techniques are necessary to increase efficiency in research and development and to train the highly skilled labor force required by the advance of technology.

5 *Increase in long-range national planning.* The time horizon used in making economic decisions is being lengthened. An important question is how far the techniques for efficient management of the economy can go and still be compatible with the traditional concept of democracy.

From Classical Liberalism to Contemporary Liberalism

Two powerful forces shaped the rise of liberalism in the eighteenth century: the rapid growth of the physical sciences and the aspirations of the members of the business class who actively promoted the development of market capitalism. The rationalism of the physical sciences was taken as the model of liberalism. There was a desire to substitute "natural order" for the seemingly arbitrary and irrational economic and social arrangements that men had contrived. It was precisely these economic and social arrangements that galled the emerging middle class. The merchants and manufacturers who came into their own with the Industrial Revolution wanted to live in a society in which there was peace and order. They wanted free production and trade and business activities to be looked upon as normal and necessary, rather than marginal and disreputable.

The central proposition of liberalism was opposition to unlimited power, particularly governmental power. According to the liberal creed, the government's main function was to uphold the liberty, equality, and security of all citizens. Centralized political power was considered dangerous because it could be used by government officials to reduce the degree of individual freedom. Consequently a basic liberal idea was that that government was best which governed least. Underlying this idea were the social values of democracy, freedom, equality, and individualism.

The ends of liberalism have remained constant since the seventeenth century, but the means have changed. Today we have two brands of liberalism, the one just described—classical liberalism—and its modern counterpart—contemporary liberalism. They hold different views of the relation between the individual and society. According to classical liberalism, the individual and society are separate and antithetical, and the former is considered to be antecedent to the latter. Contemporary liberalism conceives of human nature as in large measure the product of the social environment. Thus the individual and society are two different dimensions of the same phenomenon—human life—and one cannot exist without the other.

This difference in interpretation of the relation between the individual and society is at the root of the basic issue that separates classical and contemporary liberalism—the degree to which there should be collective control over individual behavior. To put it another way, to what extent should individual interests be subordinated to social purposes? The classical liberal point of view is that individual behavior should never be controlled by collective behavior and that individual interests should never be subordinated to social interests. The contemporary liberal point of view is that in modern mass society individuals must rely on groups and organizations to protect and further their interests. Therefore, it is not a question of subordinating the interests of individuals to those of groups and organizations so much as it is one of the extent to which groups and organizations shall be used to further individual interest.

This difference in viewpoint is seen most clearly in the classical and contemporary liberal concept of the role of the government in economic activity. The classical liberal is unalterably opposed to the expansion of government in any shape, with the exception, perhaps, of national defense. Since he considers society to be antithetical to individual welfare, he wants to limit the government as an instrument of society in size, scope, and function. He lauds private enterprise with its emphasis on individual initiative and responsibility, and he considers governmental intervention in economic activity to be dangerous and unwarranted. The contemporary liberal looks upon the Federal government as a positive instrument to help achieve the present-day economic goals of liberalism. He is not opposed to private enterprise, but he does not place as much reliance on it as the classical liberal, and he believes in supplementing it with governmental economic activity wherever necessary.

Conservatism as we know it in America today is closely related to classical liberalism. The values and beliefs of the two are quite similar. Conservatives believe just as strongly in limited government, private enterprise, and individual initiative and responsibility as do classical liberals. The difference between them is in their underlying philosophical orientations. Liberalism has always been a form of protest against powerful established interests that stand in the way of human progress. This is true of both classical and contemporary liberalism. However, conservatism by its very nature supports the status quo. It is concerned with preserving the best achievements of the past against reckless social experiments in the name of progress. Thus although classical liberals and conservatives support the same values, principles, and goals, they do so out of different motives. The former advocate a new social order that is less imperfect than the old one; the latter want to preserve an existing social order that is less imperfect than a new one would be. Nineteenth-century classical liberalism has become twentieth-century conservatism.

The trend of public economic policy since the Great Depression has been overwhelmingly in the direction of contemporary liberalism. The Truman Fair Deal consolidated the New Deal economic measures and adapted them to the post-World War II situation. The Employment Act of 1946 strengthened the hand of the executive branch in planning and coordinating economic programs to attain the goal of full employment.

Eisenhower's election in 1952 was hailed by classical liberals and conservatives as a return to pre-New Deal economic doctrines and policies; but the new administration found that once social welfare and social economic planning measures are on the statute books, they become noncontroversial and it is politically unwise to jettison them. As Calvin Hoover said, "The Eisenhower administration, having inherited the evolutionary transformation of the organization and control of industry which gave rise to the New Deal and Fair Deal and having accepted most of the economic measures of the New Deal and Fair Deal, in its actual economic policies signalized the permanence of the changed economic system."[8]

The economic philosophy of the Kennedy New Frontier was that of contemporary liberalism. In a 1962 address Kennedy said, "I am suggesting that the problems of fiscal and monetary policy in the sixties as opposed to the kinds of problems we faced in the thirties demand subtle challenges for which technical answers—not political answers—must be provided. . . . They cannot be solved by incantations from the forgotten past."[9] Johnson's vision of the Great Society continued the trend toward contemporary liberalism with new measures such as the antipoverty program, designed to further reduce inequality and provide economic security for all groups.

Despite the triumph of contemporary liberalism as the philosophical basis of postwar public economic policy, it is less well understood as an ideology than classical liberalism. There are two reasons for this. First, ideologies are inherently conservative and resist change. Classical liberalism was strongly entrenched in America for generations, and it will not be replaced without a fight. Some of the strength it has lost because of the demise of *laissez faire* has been replaced by the support it now receives from conservatives.

Second, to fully understand and accept contemporary liberalism involves facing up to the conflict between materialism and idealism in the American value system. This is an unpleasant confrontation for most Americans. We would rather believe that our values, goals, and efforts are completely integrated and pulling in the same direction. Such is not the case, however. If we had wanted the idealistic existence that Jefferson or Thoreau advocated, we would not have industrialized. We did so because we want the creature comforts as well as freedom. Classical liberalism underemphasizes the materialism in American culture because of its pseudoreligious air that harkens back to the concept of natural law. Contemporary liberalism accepts the materialistic values and goals on an equal footing with the idealistic values and goals and attempts to achieve a balance between them.

Nonetheless, it appears inevitable that contemporary liberalism will become the prevailing ideology in America. There is a gap between principle and practice in American life that is becoming more noticeable all the time. Our traditional interpretations of freedom, equality, justice, and progress were developed in the agrarian society of the seventeenth and eighteenth centuries. They are becoming increasingly out of phase with the realities of twentieth-century industrial life. When principle and practice do not jibe, it is necessary to change one or the other or develop a new way of relating the two. We cannot give up either our traditional principles or our industrial way of life. The gap between the two must be bridged by a reinterpretation of what the principles mean that is consistent with the practices. That is the ideological challenge we face, and the evolution of contemporary liberalism is the way we are most likely to meet it.

The Place of Big Business in Contemporary Liberalism

Public opinion about big business is ambiguous. People like what big business can do *for* them, but they are fearful of what it might do *to* them. This attitude came through clearly in a public opinion study of what a carefully selected national sample of 1,227 adults thinks about big business:[10]

> There seems to be considerable evidence that the American public's attitude toward "big business" is confused and superficially inconsistent. However, an internal logic is equally apparent. People like to buy cheap, they appreciate the availability of mass-produced goods, they are grateful for big industrial power in wartime; but many also seem to be distrustful of centralized, uncontrolled power and are unhappy with industry-union relations.

In other words, people may be uncomfortable about big business, but they will live with it because they desire its fruits. As long as most Americans believe that big business is the economic basis of the affluent society, apparently they will not reject it.

The ambivalence of attitude toward big business also is shown in a study in which 1,923 teen-agers in forty-two cities were interviewed. Nearly one-third of the interviewees thought of big business negatively as a form of giant monopoly. They feared that free enterprise will be a thing of the past in a few decades after small business is forced out of the economy. Most of the teen-agers were hostile in some degree toward big business, and yet almost all of the boys looked forward to becoming part of it. According to a newspaper account of the survey:[11]

Only one out of eight young men in high school expects or has any desire to go into business for himself. The majority hopes to find security and success in positions with important national companies. The "reach out for the sky" dream of American youth seems to have suffered a setback in the period since the end of World War II. Young men would rather put their trust in management of large concerns than set out on their own.

At the root of the public's concern about big business is the issue of power. We link power to bigness and bigness to un-Americanism and a loss of political control by the democratic process. The specter of corporate giants answering to nobody but themselves is a frightening one to the average person, even if he does not think that the vast power in the hands of big-business managers has so far been seriously abused. The fear is that such concentrated power *might* be used illegitimately and the public would be powerless to do anything about it. The people are supposed to be sovereign in a democracy, but they have no direct control over the managerial elite which guides the destiny of big business. Americans, therefore, are naturally suspicious of big business: It seems to be beyond their control, but it can and does control their own behavior.

This ambivalence about big business is reflected in the evolving body of contemporary liberalism. The attitude of some contemporary liberals toward big business is comparable to that of the classical liberals toward government in the nineteenth century. Michael Reagan takes the position that while concentration of power is inevitable in industrial society, big-business power and influence go far beyond what is healthy in a democratic society. He favors an expansion of government economic control and closer regulation of big-business practices.[12] Harry Girvetz recognizes the need for large-scale enterprises but believes that private power must be transformed and legitimized:

> The vast power now enjoyed by the managers and owners of large-scale enterprise should either be effectively controlled or, if this is impossible, actually wielded by responsible public officials subject to removal if their conduct is not in accord with the public interest. The same experts who now turn the wheels of industry must necessarily continue to turn them, but in response to policies either controlled or dictated by ac-

countable public officials, policies determined by law-making bodies after open hearing and not by bankers behind a door marked "Private."[13]

Another group of contemporary liberals has a much more favorable attitude toward big business and management power. Adolf Berle's books point out that traditional notions of how corporate power is checked are archaic. Major corporations finance their activities from internal sources and, therefore, are no longer checked by the judgment of the security market. Neither is their power checked by competition in the traditional sense. But this is not a cause of serious concern, Berle contends, because new checks have developed in the form of the leadership struggle in oligopolistic markets and the force of public opinion.[14] John Galbraith bridges the gap between traditional market competition and these newer constraints in his theory of countervailing power. Any power bloc behaves in such a way as to facilitate the growth of a new power bloc which becomes counterpoised against it. Thus the concentrated power of producers evoked and now is balanced by a corresponding concentration of power among large-scale distributors and nationwide labor unions.[15]

The American Attitude toward Power

Which view of big business is likely to become firmly rooted in contemporary liberalism? The answer to this question depends upon the nature of the American attitude toward power and the solution which we develop to the problem of concentrated power in industrial and democratic society. As we have seen, the outstanding characteristic of this attitude is the fear of the improper use of centralized power. Gorer, in his analysis of power in American society, says Americans believe that "authority over people is morally detestable and should be resisted, that the suspicion that others are seeking authority cannot be too vigilant, and that those who occupy the necessary positions of authority within the state should be considered as potential enemies and usurpers."[16] Galbraith has pointed out the ambiguous position of power in American society. He says that the existence of power is bound to present problems for a community "which abhors is existence, disavows its possession, but values its exercise."[17] "The privilege of controlling the actions or of affecting the income and property of other persons is something that no one of us can profess to seek or admit to possessing."[18]

What Robert Lynd calls "this American combination of ambivalence and reticence about power"[19] presents problems of adjustment in modern mass society. The high degree of interdependence of industrial society makes indispensable the centralization of sufficient power to accomplish essential social objectives. As Lynd says, "Many things must be done collectively because they can no longer be done so well—or well enough to be socially dependable—individually and piecemeal."[20] Talcott Parsons points out that a necessary condition for the effective functioning of a dynamic, pluralistic, and largely unplanned society is the recognition by members of the society that power is legitimate whenever it is needed to accomplish approved goals or preserve social values. He thinks that Americans have a practical attitude toward power, accepting its necessity for "specific approved goals but repudiating any suggestion of generalized hierarchical superiority."[21]

The traditional American public policy toward power is based on the principle of checks and balances. This policy is our solution to the conflict presented by the fact that we deplore power but accept the need for it. The purpose of checks and balances is to contain power blocs so that they are prevented from undertaking actions which lead to drastic changes in the laws and institutions of our society. Power centers could be used, if allowed complete freedom, to initiate changes so great that they would threaten the continuity and security of other parts of society. If the influence of each power bloc is checked and balanced by the other concentrations of power within society, however, overall social security and stability are safeguarded.

Therefore, we believe that political and economic power should be kept separate so that each acts as a constraint on the influence of the other. The electorate is the ultimate source of political power, but in mass society extensive powers must be delegated to those who perform the political function of governing. The principle of checks and balances provides that delegated political power must not become joined with any other kind of power (hence the continuing emphasis on the separation of church and state). This is why democratic socialism is not likely to take root in America; it would concentrate both political and economic power in the same hands. Only a relationship between political and economic power which keeps them separate can be compatible with the American attitude toward power.

The difference in the relationship between political and economic power is the crux of the ideological struggle between American capitalism and Russian communism. It is no longer sensible to think that the nature of ownership distinguishes these two systems. Private ownership of capital was abolished outright in Russia, and it has been eroded away in America by the separation of ownership and management. The really significant issue is control, not ownership. Political and economic power are collectivized in both systems, but in America political and economic power are kept as separate as possible consistent with what are considered the minimum requirements of economic health, and in Russia political and economic power (and all other forms of power) are combined in the hands of the ruling group.

Granted that the essence of contemporary industrial capitalism is the separation of concentrated political and economic power, it remains to be determined why management is allocated so much economic power. Is this the best approach to the solution of divided power? Could not economic power be allocated to some group other than management to better purpose?

The desire to make the stockholders the locus of economic power dies hard. Ever since the debate between Dodd and Berle on the question of "for whom are the managers trustees?"[22] there have been repeated exhortations to managers to look to the stockholders for their ultimate source of authority. But the fact of the matter is that the great number of stockholders is inconsistent with the need of American industrial society for a strong economic power bloc to counteract the highly centralized political power of government. When power is highly dispersed, it loses its potency.

This basic fact about power is not taken into consideration by writers who emphasize the similarities between political and economic power. They argue that if democracy works in political life, why not in economic life? This tenuous analogy is the blanket which covers such strange bedfellows as G. D. H. Cole ("industrial democracy"), Adolf Berle ("the economic republic"), and the Advertising Council ("people's capitalism").[23] There are two reasons why these approaches cannot be successful. First, they call for a degree of decentralization of power which is inconsistent with the realities of the task of managing large and complex economic units. Second, if political means are employed to coordinate the dispersed economic power through some sort of republican form of organization, state support would probably be required; and the principle

The moral crisis in management

of checks and balances would be violated. If no state support were solicited, a state within a state would be established; and the larger political system would have to liquidate its rival in order to maintain its claim to sole sovereignty.

The conclusion of this line of reasoning is that management power is legitimate, but not for the reason usually given. The idea that the power of managers is legitimate because they are trustees for the owners is a social convention which is accepted because it has the sanction of historical usage. But the real basis for the legitimacy of management power is the traditional American policy toward power of checks and balances. If the American value system is to be preserved and if we are not to give up the fruits of industrialism, it is essential that management be given sufficient power to countervail against the highly concentrated political power of the government.

Social Responsibility and Contemporary Liberalism

Our main concern with economic ideology is to determine whether the doctrine of socially responsible management is compatible with it. The analysis of this chapter has indicated that contemporary liberalism is the emerging ideology of modern capitalism. Let us now turn to the question of the relation between contemporary liberalism and the doctrine of socially responsible management. The crux of this relation, which we will examine, is the possible contribution of the social responsibility ethic to the approach toward social economic control implied in contemporary liberalism.

The laissez-faire approach of classical liberalism clearly is no longer an economic reality or possibility. Thus the old liberal dilemma of how to achieve social order in a way compatible with the inherent dignity of the individual has returned in a new form. The solution of Reagan and Girvetz and other contemporary liberals who lean toward government as the coordinating institution of society is to achieve the economic order required for economic freedom through an expansion of social economic planning. The solution of Berle and Galbraith, which calls for an important but limited role for government and reliance on private power blocs counterpoised against each other and against government, is more in line with the traditional American principle of checks and balances. It appears likely to become accepted as a key concept in the prevailing political and economic ideology. The question to which we now must address ourselves is, "How does the social responsibility ethic fit into this approach toward social control of economic activity?"

There is little doubt that the rise of big business led to a decline in price competition. But this does not necessarily mean that there has been a slackening in the social control of business. Indeed, there are theoretical and empirical reasons for believing this not to be the case. It seems highly unlikely, on theoretical grounds, that society would relinquish control over such a fundamental social institution as big business. It is the basic and indispensable structural unit of the industrial economy. In addition, it is a functioning social system in its own right. It has values, goals, and objectives which stem from its own organizational and technological needs. Many of these values, goals, and objectives are bureaucratically oriented and are in conflict with the liberal orientation of capitalism. Therefore, it is essential that industrial society control the large corporation if capitalism is to be preserved.

The empirical reason for believing that society controls big business is the surprising fact that the momentous structural changes wrought by the rise of big business seem to have had little or no effect on aggregate economic performance. The horrendous consequences of a "world of monopolies" predicted by neoclassical economic theory simply have not occurred. The most useful indicators of performance of the total economy show no changes directly traceable to changes in market structure brought about by the rise of big business. Mason has pointed out that the rate of growth of national income is not very different from what it was before 1900; the relation of labor to nonlabor incomes before taxes is about what it was before World War I; and significant changes in the distribution of personal disposable income are primarily the result of tax changes. "The broad look reveals very substantial elements of stability in the system."[24]

How can this be? A likely explanation is that while market performance is related to market structure and market structure determines the degree of competition, market competition is not the only form of social control over economic activity. As the degree of competition has declined because of the growth of big business, it apparently has been supplemented by other mechanisms of social control. Just as there is more than one enterprise objective that influences management decisions, so there is more than a single mechanism that controls the individuals and organizations that exercise control over economic resources. This, doubtless, has always been the case; but as long as competition was effective, there was little need for other control devices to become operative. Economists were able to speak with great authority about social control of business because of the refined market models they developed based on competition.

There are basically six mechanisms of social control of economic activity: the market system, organizational coordination, industrial pluralism, economic planning, cultural norms affecting the individual, and the creation and destruction of economic organizations by society. The market system includes competition between sellers and the influence that buyers bring to bear on sellers. Organizational coordination refers to the control over resources within the individual enterprise. Industrial pluralism is the system by which organized economic interest groups control each other's economic activities by gaining the political power of the state and changing the economic "rules of the game" to their own advantage. Economic planning involves the centralized control over economic resources based on political power and organization. Cultural norms—the general patterns of behavior learned by members of a society—control economic activity by prescribing what is desirable and undesirable in economic life. Social organizations are expendable: Control over economic activity by creating and destroying the organizational type that controls resources is an indirect but devastating form of control.

Each of these control mechanisms is constantly operative in some degree in every industrial economy. The particular balance between them that is employed depends upon the general orientation of the society toward social control, the economic goals of the society, and the structure of the economy. The various control mechanisms are hierarchically organized according to their degree of generality. When there is a breakdown in control at one level in the hierarchy, a more generalized device operating in a larger and more inclusive control system is brought into play.

In America we favor informal and nonauthoritarian mechanisms of social control. Freedom is equated with "*control by diffuse cultural structure rather than by a definite social organization.*"[25] It is natural, therefore, that we looked first to the market system as our basic form of social control of economic activity. When the effectiveness of this control mechanism declined because of the concentration of economic power in big business, we moved halfheartedly to the more general control mechanism of economic planning and attempted to shore up competition through antitrust regulation. But because of our belief in the advantages of big business and our reluctance to engage in overt economic planning, we have not been willing to use antitrust regulation to break up big business and restore the competitive economic structure of an earlier era. Therefore, it has become necessary to take recourse to the control mechanisms of industrial pluralism and the cultural norms governing economic behavior.

Industrial pluralism is a form of economic power relationship in which each of the major economic interest groups contends in an open bid for political power to protect and further its interests. It is based on the principle of checks and balances: "The power of the state is limited by the power of organized public opinion and large special interest groups; the pressure exercised by business interests is counterbalanced by the forces of organized labor; both management and labor must take into account the interests of an integrated consumers' movement and other public agencies."[26] The increasing reliance placed by individuals on economic interest groups in our organizational society is responsible for the "politicizing" of modern economic life. Whether this is unfortunate, as Boulding thinks, or not, the fact remains that when market controls declined there was something to fill the void.

A variety of specific cultural norms have a directing influence on economic activity. By means of laws, rules, and customs, society can shape and mold the actions of many separate individuals into a coordinated economic system that functions to a remarkable degree without overt administrative actions. "The whole economic order, looked at sociologically, is a network of norms and expectancies—a web of 'promises' as to the course that economic action will take, or is supposed to take."[27] Without this normative network, the other three control mechanisms would not be possible (e.g., market competition without rules is inconceivable; for organizational coordination to be effective the authority relations in organizations must conform to the accepted norms of interpersonal relationships; social economic planning is possible only if it is consistent with cultural norms of the proper functions of the state).

There is, however, a separate control system based on cultural norms—the system of social roles. One of the most powerful mechanisms of social control over corporate economic activity is society's capacity to delineate the social role of the manager. Once their role is clear to managers, they readily attempt to conform to it. The difficulty is that in a democratic society such as ours, with no definite and concrete goals except perhaps a generalized desire for more of the same good things of life that most of us already enjoy, expectations for such an important role are not very explicit. But the lack of clarity of the managerial role should not be interpreted to mean that this control device is weak and inconsequential. The many articles and speeches of managers about social responsibility in management attest to the imperative need of modern professional managers to come to grips with this nebulous but powerful constraint on their behavior.

When the doctrine of socially responsible management is widely understood and accepted, it will play an important role in the contemporary liberal approach to social control of big business. The American economy is still capitalistic because it protects and furthers liberal goals and values. But because of the rise of big business and the decline of competition, a new solution must be found to the problem of a source of economic order compatible with individual dignity. Industrial pluralism is an acceptable control mechanism, but it cannot do the entire job because it operates on groups, not individuals. The social responsibility ethic is effective at the level of the individual. It influences his behavior in a way that conforms with liberal values. The individual's conscience is the source of order rather than an external coercive force. When society desires a change in managerial behavior, the role of the manager is altered. The manager responds in a seemingly voluntary fashion. There is no need for overt coercion or force. Each manager does what is socially correct because he has learned that this is what he should do. The control mechanism has become internalized.

The conclusion, then, is that the doctrine of social responsibility is compatible with contemporary liberalism. When the latter is widely accepted as the economic ideology of today, it will provide solid support for the doctrine of social responsibility and the social responsibility ethic.

NOTES

1 George Stigler, "The Case against Big Business," *Fortune,* vol. 45, part 2 (May, 1952), p. 123.
2 Joe S. Bain, "Economies of Scale, Concentration and the Condition of Entry in Twenty Manufacturing Industries," *American Economic Review,* vol. 44, no. 1 (March, 1954), pp. 15–39.

3 Werner Sombart, "Capitalism," *Encyclopedia of the Social Sciences,* vol. III (New York: The Macmillan Company, 1930), pp. 195–208.

4 Karl Polanyi, *The Great Transformation* (New York: Holt, Rinehart and Winston, Inc., 1944), p. 132.

5 Arthur Schweitzer, "Theories of Controlled Capitalism," *Kyklos,* vol. 9, no. 4 (November, 1956), p. 505.

6 Bruno Seidel, *Industrialismus und Kapitalismus* (Meisenheim/Glan: Verlag Anton Hain, 1955), p. 95.

7 Andrew Shonfield, "Is Capitalism a Success?" *Encounter,* vol. 24, no. 6 (June, 1965), pp. 15–16. (Italics supplied.)

8 Calvin B. Hoover, *The Economy, Liberty and the State* (Garden City, N.Y.: Doubleday & Company, Inc., 1961), p. 270.

9 John F. Kennedy, "The Myth and Reality in Our National Economy," *Vital Speeches,* vol. 28, no. 19 (July 15, 1962).

10 B. R. Fisher and S. B. Withey, *Big Business as the People See It* (Ann Arbor, Mich.: University of Michigan Survey Research Center, 1951), p. 4.

11 Article based on the survey, *St. Louis Post-Dispatch* (Oct. 5, 1956).

12 Michael D. Reagan, *The Managed Economy* (Fair Lawn, N.J.: Oxford University Press, 1963).

13 Harry K. Girvetz, *The Evolution of Liberalism* (New York: Collier Books, Crowell-Collier Publishing Co., 1963), p. 281.

14 Adolf A. Berle, Jr., *The 20th Century Capitalist Revolution* (New York: Harcourt, Brace & World, Inc., 1954), pp. 52–58.

15 John K. Galbraith, *American Capitalism: The Concept of Countervailing Power* (Boston: Houghton Mifflin Company, 1952).

16 Geoffrey Gorer, *The American People* (New York: W. W. Norton & Company, Inc., 1948), p. 30.

17 Galbraith, *op. cit.,* p. 30.

18 *Ibid.,* p. 28.

19 Robert S. Lynd, "Power in American Society as Resource and Problem," in Arthur Kornhauser (ed.), *Problems of Power in American Democracy* (Detroit: Wayne State University Press, 1957), p. 7.

20 *Ibid.,* p. 12.

21 Talcott Parsons, "Authority, Legitimation, and Political Action," in Carl J. Friedrich (ed.), *Authority* (Cambridge, Mass.: Harvard University Press, 1958), p. 200.

22 E. Merrick Dodd, Jr., "For Whom Are Corporate Managers Trustees?" *Harvard Law Review,* vol. 45 (1932), pp. 1145–1157; Adolf Berle, Jr., "For Whom Corporate Managers *Are* Trustees," *Harvard Law Review,* vol. 45 (1932), pp. 1365–1367.

23 G. D. H. Cole, *The Case for Industrial Partnership* (New York: St. Martin's Press, Inc., 1957); Adolf A. Berle, Jr., *The American Economic Republic* (New York: Harcourt, Brace & World, Inc., 1963); and The American Round Table, *People's Capitalism* (New Haven, Conn.: The Advertising Council and Yale University, 1956).

24 Edward S. Mason, "The Apologetics of 'Managerialism,'" *Journal of Business,* vol. 31, no. 1 (January, 1958), p. 10.

25 Robin M. Williams, Jr., *American Society* (New York: Alfred A. Knopf, Inc., 1957), p. 419.

26 Gerard DeGre, "Freedom and Social Structure," *American Sociological Review,* vol. 2, no. 5 (October, 1946), p. 535.

27 Williams, *op. cit.,* p. 140.

6

Social Responsibility and Economic Theory

A business ethic must be compatible with economic theory, as well as economic ideology, to be widely accepted. The theory of the firm is the division of economic theory dealing with the motivation and behavior of the firm and manager. In its traditional form it is not compatible with the doctrine and ethic of social responsibility. Many economists are dissatisfied with the theory of the firm, however, because of the unrealistic assumptions upon which it is based. Modifications and revisions which put the theory into closer touch with reality are moving it toward a general theory of the firm in which the concept of social responsibility has a legitimate place. This chapter analyzes two lines of thought that integrate social responsibility into the theory of the firm. The first views social responsibility in terms of utility maximization, and the second views it as a means of social control over the manager.

The Economic Theory of the Firm

There are five basic assumptions upon which the traditional economic theory of the firm is based:

1 *Profit maximization:* The only goal of the firm is to earn the largest possible profit.
2 *Complete rationality:* The firm rationally pursues its profit objective.
3 *Perfect knowledge:* The firm knows what its costs and revenues will be.
4 *Identity of firm and entrepreneur:* For purposes of analysis there is no difference between the firm and its owner-manager.
5 *Competition:* The only external influence on the firm's behavior is market competition.

On the basis of these assumptions, economists construct models of the real world situations in which firms function. The market structure in which the firm operates is the "given" in the model. There are five types of market structure:

1 *Perfect competition:* many sellers dealing in the same good
2 *Monopolistic competition:* many sellers dealing in similar goods
3 *Pure oligopoly:* few sellers dealing in the same good
4 *Differentiated oligopoly:* few sellers dealing in similar goods
5 *Monopoly:* one seller dealing in a good

Variables in the models (i.e., those elements that can take different values) are prices, inputs of resources, costs, and products. By relating these variables to one another within the framework of the given market structure, economists can make predictions about the number of units the firm will produce and the selling price.

The firm must determine at which of the possible combinations of price and output it will maximize profits. By definition this is where there is the greatest difference between total revenue and total costs. This price-output combination is found by using marginal analysis. If the revenue received from selling the last unit produced (marginal revenue) is greater than the cost of producing that unit (marginal cost), the level of output is too low to maximize profits. There still is additional profit to be made by expanding output. The firm maximizes profit at the output where marginal revenue equals marginal cost, and no profit is made on the last unit produced.

The market structure in which the firm operates plays a crucial role in determining the level of price and output. In a perfectly competitive market, the firm has no control over its selling price. Since many perfectly substitutable products already are available on the market, there is no chance of getting more than the going market price. On the other hand, since the firm can sell all it wants at the going market price, there is no advantage in selling for less. Therefore, the only decision to be made is at which level of output to produce. Firms in imperfectly competitive markets have some control over their prices because there are no perfect substitutes for their products. Thus they must take into account the changes in their prices and revenues which occur at various levels of output and sales. The same decision-making rule applies for them, however, as for the firms in perfectly competitive markets: Profit is maximized at that level of output where marginal revenue equals marginal cost.

A major criticism of the economic theory of the firm is that firms do not, in fact, maximize profits. Two Oxford economists, C. J. Hitch and R. L. Hall, found after examining English business practices that marginal analysis was not used in making business decisions.[1] Richard Lester came to the same conclusion on the basis of statistical study in this country. He concluded that businessmen do not consider marginal analysis to be a practical operating principle because it is too difficult to apply in the complex modern business world.[2] Robert Anthony described several business practices which are incompatible with profit maximization (e.g., separation payments for discharged workers, capital budgeting by businessmen, pricing policies).[3] Robert Gordon has emphasized the impossibility of businessmen adjusting marginally for the continuous changes that confront them and gives this as the reason why they develop shortcuts in real life situations.[4]

Other critics of the traditional theory of the firm argue that the assumption that the firm has perfect knowledge and thus operates under conditions of complete certainty is invalid. They reason that businessmen cannot know in advance which of the alternative future courses of action that are open to the firm will be most profitable. Therefore, it is necessary that the theory include decision making under conditions of risk and uncertainty. Significant progress in this direction has been made in the new economic field of decision theory, with the focus on *how* decisions are made rather than *why* they are made.[5]

A closely related theoretical development has been the application of game theory to economic behavior. The assumption that the firm is completely rational is of questionable validity in oligopolistic markets because the reaction of firms to price changes cannot be predicted. How is it possible to act rationally when the behavior patterns of others who have a bearing on the situation are unknown? Von Neumann and Morgenstern have endeavored to solve this problem by the theory of games, which is an analytical framework for establishing criteria for rational behavior in conflict situations.[6]

Natural science concepts have been borrowed by some economists to develop biological models of the firm as alternatives to the traditional economic theory of the firm. The concept of homeostasis developed by physiologist Walter Cannon has been applied to the firm by Kenneth Boulding. Cannon found that living beings tend to be in a physiological equilibrium such that, when the body is disturbed, certain adaptive responses occur to bring about a return to the homeostatic state. Boulding reasons by analogy that the firm is in a similar equilibrium situation. When its equilibrium is disturbed, forces automatically go into action to return the firm to the homeostatic state. Thus the firm is a reactive entity rather than the active one pictured in the traditional economic theory of the firm.[7] A similar approach is followed by economists who have worked in the area of "viability analysis." They want to explain why certain firms are successful over long periods of time. Armen Alchian has theorized that firms may survive through their "adaption" to the environment as well as through their "adoption" by it. Firms may adapt to the environment by copying the successful behavior of other firms.[8] Thus viability analysis is an application of Darwin's theory of natural selection and evolution to the business world.

This discussion of the theory of the firm indicates that it is being revised by introducing greater reality into the basic assumptions. The next section deals with innovations in the assumptions of profit maximization and the identity of firm and entrepreneur. These changes in assumptions make it possible to treat the concept of social responsibility as utility maximization within the framework of the economic theory of the firm.

Nonprofit Goals and Management Autonomy

In a pathbreaking article, Benjamin Higgins[9] suggested in 1939 that firms operating in markets that are not perfectly competitive have freedom to seek goals in addition to profit. The reason for this is that the entrepreneur has a margin with which to work, and he can use it to satisfy desires other than for profit. Higgins classified nonprofit goals into two groups: (1) those which lead to a lower output than at the profit-maximizing level and (2) those which lead to a greater output than at the profit-maximizing level. An example of the first category is leisure. The entrepreneur who values leisure highly will optimize at a lower level of output and profit than one who does not because he will be willing to forego some profit for greater leisure. In the second category is the desire to own a large firm for the prestige it gives, the desire to employ more labor, or the desire to expand output so that selling price can be lowered. In this case the entrepreneur will accept a lower total profit in return for an expansion of output.

Other nonprofit goals which have been put in models are entrepreneurial control of the firm and financial liquidity. Melvin Reder[10] suggested that the pursuit of profit is modified by the desire of the entrepreneur to retain control of the firm. He related present value of the firm's net worth to the average planned rate of growth of firm assets. The profit-maximizing firm is indifferent to dilution of ownership. Funds for asset expansion will be secured from whatever source necessary to attain the profit-maximizing rate of growth. When entrepreneurial control is also a goal, a constraint is placed on asset acquisition beyond the point where ownership is diluted below the level necessary to maintain control. A variation of this model by W. W. Cooper[11] defined control in terms of financial liquidity. Like Reder, he described the goal structure of firms in terms of control as well as profit, but he emphasized the importance of strong liquid assets in preserving dominant ownership in the firm. He argued that a profit-maximizing firm behaves differently from one which desires a strong cash position as well as profits.

Armen Alchian and Reuben Kessel made a significant advance in the theory of nonprofit firm goals by developing a model which included not one but several goals in addition to profit. Forerunners of this development were contained in models constructed by Martin Bronfenbrenner and Gary Becker. Bronfenbrenner[12] suggested that a firm in a monopsonistic labor market may hire at a wage rate higher than the minimum possible level in order to select workers on the basis of characteristics in addition to minimum efficiency (e.g., race, sex, religion). Becker developed the same argument independently with reference to racial discrimination. He argued that discrimination may occur in the marketplace because of race, religion, sex, color, social class, personality, or other nonpecuniary considerations. The entrepreneur is assumed to have a taste for discrimination: "When an employer discriminates against employees, he acts as if he incurs nonpecuniary, psychic costs of production by employing them."[13]

Alchian and Kessel[14] expanded Becker's argument by suggesting that entrepreneurs can introduce other tastes into firm goal systems besides discrimination (e.g., plush executive offices for management, heavy staff support for top management, generous fringe benefits for management, pretty secretaries). In short, the Alchian-Kessel model suggests that entrepreneurs maximize utility rather than profit. They argue that utility maximization is not a vague and tautological motivational assumption when the "goods" that add to utility are precisely stipulated. Their model differs from that of Higgins in that it assumes no difference in the indifference systems of entrepreneurs in competitive or monopolistic market structures. Entrepreneurs in both kinds of markets can be expected to have the same prejudices and desire for the good life on the job. However, the monopolist can transform excess profits into nonpecuniary income and therefore does not have to pay as high a price for nonprofit goals as entrepreneurs in competitive markets. The latter can ill afford to use funds for high living on the job which decreases profits essential for the firm's financial well-being.

The literature on multiple-goal firms is consistent with the assumption of the identity of firm and entrepreneur, but several recent additions to the literature analyzing the modern large corporation dispense with it. They assume a separation of ownership and control in large, widely owned corporations and recognize that most of these firms operate in oligopolistic markets where managers are free enough from the pressure of competition to choose among alternative courses of action.

This line of analysis is coming to be known as "the theory of managerial enterprise." This theory assumes that management is largely autonomous and may have goals different from those of stockholders. It analyzes the motives and goals of managers, the constraints imposed on managers of firms in oligopolistic markets, and the behavior which results. The focus is on "management as the group which impresses its goals on the corporation in the process of both making and carrying out basic corporate decisions."[15]

An important contribution, the theory of managerial enterprise by Oliver Williamson, makes use of insights provided by organization theory. The manager is a "peak coordinator" who occupies a strategic position in the firm by virtue of his access to privileged information and his concern with overall enterprise activities. In Williamson's model organizational slack is assumed to exist. It takes the form of excess staff, spending on travel, office improvements, and expense accounts. Such expenditures go beyond profit-maximizing levels and illustrate the potential conflict between the goals of owners and managers.

Williamson further develops the Alchian-Kessel idea of the taste of managers for nonpecuniary income with the concept of expense preference. This device enables him to transform nonpecuniary motives (e.g., prestige, security, power) into pecuniary terms. By expense preference he means "that managers do not have a neutral attitude toward all classes of expense."[16] Some types of expenses have positive values and are incurred because they enhance managerial nonprofit objectives. Thus nonpecuniary goals are assumed to influence the firm's operations in systematic and predictable ways. Managers are assumed to possess expense preferences for expansion of staff because security goals are enhanced; and for expense accounts, office improvements, and philanthropic disbursements because they give power and prestige to top executives.

R. Joseph Monsen and Anthony Downs have developed a theory of large managerial firms which also separates management from the firm.

They assume the ownership of large firms is so widely diffused that managers think of owners in the same way as they do the general public. The motivations of each group are different: Owners desire a steady income from dividends and gradual appreciation of the market price of stock; managers strive to maximize their own lifetime incomes. Since managers' incomes are not identical with the firm's profits, "when managers act in their own self-interest, they do not always act in the interest of the owners."[17] The incomes which they maximize include both monetary elements and nonmonetary elements (e.g., leisure, prestige, power).

Social Responsibility as Utility Maximization

Harold Johnson is the academic economist who has gone furthest in integrating the concept of social responsibility into the theory of the firm. He believes that economists are too ready to dismiss this concept as "bewildering balderdash" or "a glittering generality." On the basis of the work done on nonprofit goals of firms and the managerial theory of the firm, he has constructed a model which treats social responsibility as utility maximization. He is careful to point out that his analysis is in the sphere of positive rather than normative economics. His goal is to frame the concept of social responsibility in conventional economic concepts and diagrams, thereby making it more tractable and open to appraisal.

Johnson thinks there are two alternative definitions of social responsibility: "*one,* through the door of utility maximization by the entrepreneur, and *two,* by attention to social variables in the preference functions of inputs and customers."[18] In the first definition, the firm is socially responsible because that is what managers want. In the second definition, managers have learned that it pays off in profits to operate the firm in a socially responsible way. Thus Johnson distinguishes between *genuine* and *expedient adherents* to social responsibility.

Johnson bases his model on the analytical advances of Becker, Alchian and Kessel, and Williamson. Becker gave the lead, he believes, with a classification of positive and negative discrimination, separating nonpecuniary goals into those regarded as "good" and those regarded as "bad."[19] The implication of this for Johnson is that social responsibility simply means that managers pursue tastes for discrimination which are socially commendable. Thus the utility maximization treatment of prejudice against Negroes or Jews can be applied to other nonprofit variables derived from the mainstream of American values (e.g., aid to education, maintenance of safe and pleasant working conditions, support of research, contribution to local charity, employment of the handicapped). "By this definition social responsibility exists if the general preference function of the manager includes variables that coincide with what the American community regards as desirable."[20]

This interpretation is illustrated graphically by Johnson in the accompanying diagram. Profits and philanthropic contributions to education, charity, or basic research are plotted on the axes. The *TMNV* opportunity line suggests that philanthropic contributions are considered commendable in contemporary American culture. A manager having a positive expense preference for corporate charity optimizes at *N*. He is willing to trade some profits for the satisfactions of philanthropic giving. On the other hand, the astute profit maximizer may also make philanthropic contributions because he is confronted with consumers and input owners who are favorably impressed with such contributions. He finds it pays in the long run to make some contributions, and he optimizes at *M*.

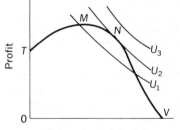

Johnson goes no further with the analysis, apparently being content to show "that the 'nonsense' idea of social responsibility can take on some meaning when couched in terms of utility maximization."[21] He finds the second or expedient-adherent approach to social responsibility more compatible with the traditional motivation of profit maximization. What it is, of course, is merely a more sophisticated version of profit maximization. Johnson does not deal with a very important question concerning the genuine adherent to social responsibility: Why does he want to be socially responsible? If he has the autonomy to choose goals which maximize his own utility, why would he select that combination which coincides with the community's general preference function? Johnson looks upon him simply as a good guy "gratifying his tastes for nonpecuniary income."[22]

A Behavioral Theory of the Firm

A fully developed theory of the firm will be a model—an abstract representation of how firms behave in the real world. Such a model will make no pretense of being a completely accurate description of reality because if it were it would defeat its own purpose. The purpose of a theoretical model is not to *describe* what happens in the real world; it is to *explain* a certain class of happenings. If a model is to be useful, it must be simplified by leaving out details that do not affect the principle of the phenomenon under study. The model is constructed by selecting a few of the key features of the real world situation and systematically relating them to create a simplified picture of reality. Therefore, in developing a theory of the firm it is necessary to select carefully the main elements and the relationships to be analyzed.

The total number of variables that influence firm behavior is very large, but they can be grouped into three logical categories. First, there are *overt actions* of firms. These are the aspects of behavior that are ordinarily considered as the objects of the decision-making process within the firm. Examples of overt actions are purchasing raw materials, producing goods, setting prices, competing with other firms, and so on. Such actions can be explained in terms of two kinds of conditions which constitute the second group of variables: the *environmental conditions* within which the firm operates and the *internal conditions* that determine how the firm functions as an organization. The third group of variables consists of "the basic physical, biological, psychological, sociological, political, and historical facts that explain the environmental and internal conditions."[23]

The behavioral sciences have a potentially great contribution to make to the development of a general theory of the firm. The nature of this contribution will be in the direction of providing an analytical framework for explaining how environmental and internal conditions affect firm behavior. The end result of this type of analysis will be a behavioral theory of the firm. A promising start in developing such a theory already has been made by the organization theorists. They have dealt with such questions as organizational viability (i.e., what relation between individuals is necessary for organizational survival), the relation between individual motives and organizational goals, and how decisions are made in organizations.

Perhaps the most significant contribution so far to the development of a behavioral theory of the firm is the volume *A Behavioral Theory of the Firm* by Richard Cyert and James March. The focus of their analysis is on the organizational decision-making process. They develop four subtheories:[24]

1. A theory of organizational goals that shows how they are formed and altered, and how they influence organizational behavior.
2. A theory of expectations that explains how organizations search for information and gather it.
3. A theory of choice that shows how organizations select alternatives and choose among them.
4. A theory of control to explain the implementation of decisions.

After the firm is conceived as an organization, the next logical step is to analyze its relations with the social environment. Papandreou, in a comprehensive survey of the theory of the firm, called attention to the fact that, "Both the goals toward which the firm strives . . . and the manner in which they are attained are subject to powerful and all-pervasive influences *from outside* the firm." These influences go beyond competition. They include "the unconscious influence provided by the mores, folklore, customs, institutions, social ideas, and myths of a society which lay the foundation for formal organizations."[25]

Neither the economic theory of the firm nor organization theory has much to say about the influence on corporate behavior of noneconomic forces in the environment of business. The corporation is conceived solely in economic terms in the economic theory of the firm, and therefore only its overt economic activities are of significance. We have seen, however, that the large corporation has a social and cultural role which can be analyzed quite apart from its economic role. The firm performs various social functions beyond producing goods and services, and it is subject to the constraints of environmental forces other than market competition. Organization theory does allow for noneconomic goals and functions of the corporation by conceiving of the corporation as an entity that adapts to its external environment. But it focuses on the internal environment of the enterprise and has little to say explicitly about how processes and conditions within the enterprise are influenced by external variables. What is needed, then, for a more comprehensive theory of the firm is a way to theoretically treat the external forces that impinge upon it and influence its behavior.

The focus of such an approach will be on the total enterprise rather than on particular parts of it or the relations of parts to each other. A behavioral theory of the firm which focuses on environmental forces will take as given the market relations that are the chief concern of the economic theory of the firm and the integrative and coordinative activities within the firm that are dealt with in organization theory. It assumes that the firm has the kind of internal structure and leadership that are necessary for it to function effectively as a unit in the market and in society at large.

This assumption makes it possible to isolate the factors that determine the nature of the relationship of the firm with its external environment. It is reasonable to treat the firm in this way—as a collective unit—because it performs the function of all organizations of acting as an intermediary between external forces and the actions and behavioral patterns of individuals, groups, and departments within it. From the environmental viewpoint, the chief function of the firm as an organizational entity is to perceive, organize, and implement the directions provided by these environmental forces so that it can perform its functions in accordance with the needs of society.

Techniques of Social Control[26]

The assumption in the economic theory of the firm that market competition is the only external force acting on the firm is invalid from the viewpoint of the behavioral theory of the firm. This assumption has withstood attacks through the years from the German historical economists, socialist theorists, the American institutionalists, and many others. But because of the increasing theoretical rigor of the behavioral sciences and the mounting evidence of nonmarket influences on the large corporation and management, this assumption also appears to be ready for modification. As Herbert Simon pointed out in his invited lecture before the

1961 annual meeting of the American Economic Association, "We are now becoming increasingly aware that the price mechanism is just one—although an exceedingly important one—of the means that humans can and do use to make rational decisions in the face of uncertainty and complexity. We are beginning to understand what some of the other mechanisms are and how they are used."[27]

The tendency of economists to conceive of the firm as the locus of social control of economic activity is misleadingly anthropomorphic. The phrase "social control of the firm" implies that the enterprise is a living entity which can control its own behavior, and this, of course, is not true. Social control is a process by which behavior is influenced to conform to some set of norms. To be effective it must act on human beings because only they can determine patterns of behavior. Organizations such as firms are abstractions—communication networks tying together social systems of men performing interrelated roles with the aid of various kinds of capital equipment. A firm is not a person except in a fictional legal sense. It cannot do the things necessary to control its own behavior: think, evaluate, make decisions, and implement policies. Only human beings do these things. Therefore, the firm cannot be controlled directly; it must indirectly be controlled through the manager, the controller of the firm.

To control a person, one must produce certain responses in him by acting on his subjective "field" of awareness. Each individual has his own special conscious and unconscious awareness of the universe. Social psychologists call this his psychological field. It is made up of the self and its relations with other objects, resources and capacities, feelings of reward and deprivation, symbols and expectations. There are basically two ways of acting on a person's field. The first is by changing his resources and capacities for rewarding or penalizing others and thus altering his expectations and responses. For example, a politician's capacity to influence foreign policy depends largely on whether he is in or out of office. The second is by influencing the person's personal expectations of rewards and deprivations. One's incentives may be altered by teaching him that a given stimulus will be followed by certain rewards and deprivations and that a particular response will avoid the deprivation and win the reward.

There are four basic techniques of social control:

1 *Spontaneous field control:* acting on another person's field without intending to do so

2 *Manipulated field control:* acting on another person's field deliberately
   in order to secure a definite response by manipulating stimuli leading
   to rewards and deprivations
3 *Command:* controlling the response of a subordinate by threatening
   him with a penalty for nonperformance (a particular case of manipulated field control)
4 *Reciprocity:* two or more people employing command or manipulated
   field control against each other

Spontaneous field control is a paradoxical technique of social control.
It is a basic control technique in all walks of life; yet many people do
not think of it as a form of control. It is the most tyrannical control
to which most people are ever subjected, but it seems compatible with
freedom. It is unintended rather than deliberate control. Therefore, it
can be pictured as the opposite of planning; yet it is one of the most
important techniques of rational social action.

How does this paradoxical control technique work? Often when a person
acts, without intending to do so he produces a stimulus about rewards
and deprivations which influences a second person. The second person
responds in an attempt to avoid the threatened deprivations or secure
the reward. Yet the first person did not deliberately set out to produce
this response. Thus the second person's response is functionally dependent
upon the original act of the first person. Unintentionally, the first person
controlled the second person's response.

Spontaneous field control is tyrannical because it is hard to escape.
Wherever one goes a network of spontaneous field controls envelops
him—in the family and among neighbors, colleagues, employees, and ac-
quaintances. Many of the rewards and deprivations dispensed by spontaneous field control are of fundamental importance to human beings (e.g.,
love and hate, affection and hostility, friendship and enmity, respect and
contempt). Anarchists might conceive of a voluntary system of social
order which substitutes spontaneous field control for state-enforced commands without recognizing its tyrannical nature. This is because it has
none of the earmarks of social control: There are no commands, regulations, statutes or laws, judicial systems, or prisons for violators.

The four techniques of social control—spontaneous field control, manipulated field control, command, and reciprocity—are operative in all
areas of society, but they are not always sufficient to bring about the

desired state of events. They act directly on the person or group to be controlled, and there are limits to the effectiveness of direct control. Therefore, it is necessary to supplement the techniques of direct social control with the following methods of roundabout control:

1 *By affecting personality:* Control can be used to change a person's personality so that a hitherto ineffectual stimulus will now lead to the desired response.
2 *By affecting roles:* A person's response to a stimulus depends largely upon the expectations of the role he is playing; thus by changing the content of the role, control can bring about a shift in responses to stimuli.

Social Responsibility as Fulfillment of the Manager Role

Of the four techniques of social control, spontaneous field control is the most compatible with the American value system. As we saw in the last chapter, we favor informal and nonauthoritarian mechanisms of social control in this country. Therefore, if a control technique is necessary, we naturally prefer a spontaneous field control rather than a command method of control because it seems least like control. For this reason we have preferred competition as the primary form of economic control; and when competition declined in significance, another form of spontaneous field control developed naturally to supplement it.

Adam Smith was the first to grasp the potentialities of economic coordination through spontaneous competitive controls. His idea of competition as the "invisible hand" better characterized his understanding of control than the "hands off" approach of *laissez faire.* In his *Wealth of Nations,* he attempted to demonstrate the superiority of the spontaneous field control of competition over the manipulated field control of command. Unfortunately his insight did not extend into other forms of spontaneous field control, and most economists ever since have closed their minds to the possibility that any others exist.

Competition when viewed as a form of spontaneous field control is a way of controlling the businessman by spontaneous alteration of his field. "As a seller, the businessman is spontaneously controlled by the possibility open to his customers to spend their funds on other products rather than accept his low price."[28] If a customer attempts to deliberately influence the seller by *threatening* to buy from someone else unless he lowers the price, this would be a case of manipulated field control. Generally, however, the buyer's control over the seller is a by-product of his ability to quietly turn from him to another seller who offers a more desirable good or a lower price. To control a seller, not all buyers need turn to substitutes. All that is required is a substantial loss of sales at the margin.

This type of spontaneous field control still exists, of course, despite the rise of big business. But the corporate and managerial revolutions have rendered it less effective than it used to be. Sales promotion, advertising, and product changes have succeeded in differentiating the seller's product sufficiently, in many cases, to reduce the range of substitute products in the buyer's field. Furthermore, in industries dominated by a few giants, prices are set by administrative decision rather than the spontaneous pricing mechanism of the market.

This study has taken the position that when competition became less effective as a spontaneous field control, it was natural that some other form of spontaneous field control developed to supplement it because of the American value orientation. To be sure, many other control techniques have been employed. Antitrust and public utility regulation have had some success as forms of command control. Public planning schemes have operated as manipulated field controls. But because of our opposition to authoritarian means of control and our dedication to control processes that are so ubiquitous and invisible that they are part of the landscape, it was highly likely that another form of spontaneous field control would develop to supplement competition.

In Chapter 4 we said the most satisfactory interpretation of social responsibility for analytical purposes is that of the manager fulfilling the expectations of his social role. It is now possible to clarify what this means. Society is a social system composed of related statuses, each of which has an associated role. The role is a cluster of norms, an interrelated set of standards of behavior which indicate how the person performing the role is expected to behave. The role player comes into contact with many other role players in many different social subsystems (e.g., the family, church, lodge, business). These other role players act on his field. Those with whom he interacts regularly exercise manipulated field control over him, and those with whom he does not interact regularly exercise spontaneous field control over him. Competitors, bankers, government officials, union leaders, and members of the board of directors exercise manipulated field control over the manager. But many others (e.g., ministers, professors, journalists, politicians, television stars, his childrens' friends) also act on his field unintentionally.

The significance of this form of spontaneous field control is that the manager is continuously exposed to incoming stimuli which give him a broad picture of what life is like in the United States and offer clues about how he is to fit into it. In short, all these incoming clues and bits of information give him some insight into the content of his role as manager. He takes this information seriously (whether he knows it or not) because it is relevant to his expectations about rewards and deprivations. If he were to go contrary to the direction of social change, he might be able to get away with it for awhile; but eventually he would lose his position, power, prestige, and income. Therefore, to be socially responsible from the behavioral point of view means to follow the dictates of society in fulfilling the obligations associated with the status of manager.

Kenneth Boulding has discussed this matter in the context of ethics. He points out that nobody can continue indefinitely in a pattern of behavior which he cannot ultimately justify to himself. "Justification, however, almost inevitably implies some larger reference outside the immediate welfare of the individual concerned: this larger reference is 'ethics' "[29] He goes on to say that cybernetic theory demands that the manager have some idea of "good performance" against which he can measure his "actual performance." "What is regarded as a good performance, however, depends on the whole impact of social communications on the formation of the role."[30] What Boulding calls social communications we have referred to as the stimuli from spontaneous field control. The problem of defining the ideal role of the manager is a difficult one, Boulding points out. There are two reasons for this. First, as we have seen, the stimuli which constitute spontaneous field control are nebulous and hard to organize into a coherent picture of reality. Second, because society is never stationary, the manager role is always in the process of being altered.

The question of why a manager chooses to be socially responsible, which was discussed earlier in connection with Johnson's interpretation of social responsibility as utility maximization, can also be raised here. If the manager is socially responsible in order to avoid deprivations and win rewards, this indeed is a form of utility maximization. But this is a short-run view. In the long run each of us is socialized to want what we get. "We start by finding a wall between us and our desires; we end by bringing our desires to our own side of the wall. We start by trying to get what we want; we end by wanting what we get. We are controlled at first by external constraints, such as the fear of punishment, and we end controlled by conscience well within the walls of our prison."[31] This suggests that managers are socially responsible because they want to be, quite apart from any monetary or other tangible rewards that are involved. Over the long run, society "manufactures" the kinds of people needed to fill important statuses. The roundabout method of control induces changes in the personalities of those occupying the status of manager; the managers react to the stimuli of spontaneous field control with the desired responses.

Comparison of the Two Approaches to Social Responsibility

The two economic approaches to social responsibility can be compared in terms of:

1 The assumptions of the economic theory of the firm they modify
2 Their empirical verifiability
3 Their compatibility with economic theory

As we saw early in the chapter, each of the assumptions of the traditional economic theory of the firm has been challenged and modified in recent years. The utility-maximization approach to social responsibility modified the assumption of profit maximization. But it also is based on a modification of the assumption of the identity of the firm and entrepreneur. The view of social responsibility as fulfillment of the manager role modified the assumption that competition is the only external influence on the firm. It too is based on the notion of the separation of the manager and the firm. Each approach derives its particular quality from the assumption which it modifies. The utility-maximization approach views social responsibility in terms of the theory of managerial choice; the role-fulfillment approach views it in terms of the theory of social control.

The role-fulfillment approach appears more susceptible to empirical economic analysis than the utility-maximization approach. Johnson's analysis ends with the conclusion that a socially responsible manager will attempt to maximize a set of those variables which the American community regards as desirable. But we do not know why a manager wants to be socially responsible. Presumably there is something in his personality makeup which leads to this kind of behavior, but personality variables are notoriously inaccessible to economic analysis. The role-fulfillment approach, however, views social responsibility as a form of economic control which comes into play when competition decreases. Since the level of competition is functionally related to market structure, it should be possible to predict the conditions under which a manager will behave in a socially responsible way (e.g., *ceteris paribus* managers of large firms in oligopolistic markets will be more socially responsible than managers of small firms in competitive markets).

The utility-maximization approach fits in more neatly with the traditional concepts and graphics of economics than the role-fulfillment approach. As we saw, there has been a clear line of evolution of utility maximization in economic journals beginning with Higgins' article in 1939 and ending with Johnson's in 1966. The role-fulfillment approach, on the other hand, is novel. Role theory has not yet been accepted as a tool of economic analysis. Yet it is bound to be a powerful concept in a fully developed behavioral theory of the firm. When such a theory does develop, it will offer strong support to the doctrine and ethic of social responsibility.

NOTES

1   C. J. Hitch and R. L. Hall, "Price Theory and Business Behavior," *Oxford Economic Papers* (May, 1939).

2   Richard A. Lester, "Shortcomings of Marginal Analysis for Wage-Employment Problems," *American Economic Review,* vol. 36, no. 1 (March, 1946).

3   Robert N. Anthony, "The Trouble with Profit Maximization," *Harvard Business Review,* vol. 38, no. 6 (November–December, 1960).

4   Robert A. Gordon, "Short-period Price Determination in Theory and Practice," *American Economic Review,* vol. 38, no. 3 (June, 1948).

5   For a review of the literature in decision theory see Joseph W. McGuire, *Theories of Business Behavior* (Englewood Cliffs, N.J.: Prentice-Hall, Inc., 1960), chap. 6.

6 John Von Neumann and Oskar Morgenstern, *Theory of Games and Economic Behavior* (Princeton, N.J.: Princeton University Press, 1944).

7 Kenneth E. Boulding, *A Reconstruction of Economics* (New York: John Wiley & Sons, Inc., 1950).

8 Armen A. Alchian, "Uncertainty, Evolution and Economic Theory," *Journal of Political Economy,* vol. 58, no. 3 (June, 1950).

9 Benjamin Higgins, "Elements of Indeterminacy in the Theory of Non-Perfect Competition," *American Economic Review,* vol. 29, no. 3 (September, 1939), pp. 468–479.

10 Melvin Reder, "A Reconsideration of Marginal Productivity Theory," *Journal of Political Economy,* vol. 55, no. 5 (October, 1947), pp. 450–458.

11 W. W. Cooper, "Theory of the Firm: Some Suggestions for Revision," *American Economic Review,* vol. 49, no. 6 (December, 1949), pp. 1204–1222.

12 Martin Bronfenbrenner, "Potential Monopsony in Labor Markets," *Industrial and Labor Relations Review,* vol. 9, no. 4 (July, 1956), pp. 577–588.

13 Gary S. Becker, *The Economics of Discrimination* (Chicago: The University of Chicago Press, 1957), p. 122.

14 Armen A. Alchian and Reuben A. Kessel, "Competition, Monopoly and the Pursuit of Money," in *Aspects of Labor Economics: A Conference* (Princeton, N.J.: Princeton University Press, 1962), pp. 157–183.

15 William L. Baldwin, "The Motives of Managers, Environmental Restraints, and the Theory of Managerial Enterprise," *Quarterly Journal of Economics,* vol. 78, no. 2 (May, 1964), p. 239.

16 Oliver Williamson, *The Economics of Discretionary Behavior: Managerial Objectives in the Theory of the Firm* (Englewood Cliffs, N.J.: Prentice-Hall, Inc., 1964), p. 33.

17 R. Joseph Monsen, Jr., and Anthony Downs, "A Theory of Large Managerial Firms," *Journal of Political Economy,* vol. 73, no. 3 (June, 1965), p. 226.

18 Harold L. Johnson, "Graphic Analysis of Multiple-goal Firms: Development, Current Status and Critique," Occasional Paper no. 5, Center for Research, College of Business Administration, Pennsylvania State University (April, 1966), p. 27.

19 Becker, *op. cit.,* p. 7.

20 Johnson, *op. cit.,* p. 27.

21 *Ibid.,* p. 30.

22 Harold L. Johnson, "Socially Responsible Firms: An Empty Box or a Universal Set?" *Journal of Business,* vol. 39, no. 3 (July, 1966), p. 399.

23 Howard R. Bowen, *The Business Enterprise as a Subject for Research* (New York: Social Science Research Council, 1955), p. 2.

24 Richard M. Cyert and James G. March, *A Behavioral Theory of the Firm* (Englewood Cliffs, N.J.: Prentice-Hall, Inc., 1963).

25 Andreas G. Papandreou, "Some Basic Problems in the Theory of the Firm," in Bernard F. Haley (ed.), *A Survey of Contemporary Economics,* vol. II (Homewood, Ill.: Richard D. Irwin, Inc., 1952), p. 192.

26 This section is based on Robert A. Dahl and Charles E. Lindblom, *Politics, Economics and Welfare* (New York: Harper & Row, Publishers, Incorporated, 1953), pp. 97–111.

27 Herbert A. Simon, "New Developments in the Theory of the Firm," *American Economic Review, Papers and Proceedings,* vol. 52, no. 2 (May, 1962), p. 14.

28 Dahl and Lindblom, *op. cit.,* p. 178.

29 Kenneth E. Boulding, "The Present Position of the Theory of the Firm," in Kenneth E. Boulding and W. Allen Spivey (eds.), *Linear Programming and the Theory of the Firm* (New York: The Macmillan Company, 1960), p. 16.

30 *Ibid.,* p. 16.

31 *Ibid.,* p. 17.

Status and Function of Corporation and Manager

Chapter 4 pointed out that criticisms of the doctrine and ethic of social responsibility fall into the four fairly well-defined problem areas of the status, function, power, and control of the corporation and manager, and that these problems must be solved before the doctrine and ethic can become widely accepted. Chapters 5 and 6 have dealt with the problems of power and control of corporations and managers. This chapter deals with the problem of the status and function of corporations and managers.

Evolving Status of the Corporation

A brief examination of the historical evolution of the corporation indicates that it has not always been a strictly economic entity and its position has shifted considerably. In the several hundred years during which the corporation has been a legally sanctioned form of social organization, its essential reason for existence has remained unchanged although the uses to which it has been put and its relationship with the state have passed through several phases. Corporations come into being because of the desire to give individuality to the actions of a group of individuals acting in concert. Individuals must perform the actions attributable to the corporation, but they do so in the name of the corporation. It creates a common action where no common action is otherwise possible.

Although the business enterprise is the most familiar type of corporation today, it was a comparatively late development in the evolution of the corporation. The first corporations of the modern era were established in England and Western Europe late in the Middle Ages when the institutions of feudalism were under assault. Municipal boroughs and craft and mercantile guilds were organized as corporations outside of the feudal system and in opposition to it. These innovations in social organization were necessary to meet new social needs. Groups of individuals needed to act as a unit in order to protect and promote their common interests. The control over members offered by the corporate organization enabled the group to limit the conditions of individual activity and prevent individual gain at the expense of the group. In a period when life was static and narrowly circumscribed geographically, it was quite natural for corporate activity to take such expression. The use of the corporation positively as a means of affording expression to unified activity was of secondary importance.

The business corporation developed in England in the sixteenth and seventeenth centuries as a means of furthering the policies of mercantilism, and it departed from its predecessors in important ways. The mercantile corporation represented a fusion of the concept of a group legal entity and the process of stock trading. Its purposes were external to the incorporating group. The corporation was a necessary means of collecting sufficient capital to undertake economic ventures too large for individuals or families, such as foreign trading, colonization, and privateering. A monopoly privilege usually accompanied the granting of a corporate charter, and therefore the corporation exercised privileges as a unit rather than administered privileges and regulations among its members as the medieval corporation had done. The close relations among members which had characterized the medieval corporations did not exist among the investors in mercantile corporations. Consequently the self-government of the former no longer had functional significance, and, eventually it was discarded and the business of the corporation was conducted by a few of the leading shareholders.

As the medieval corporation changed to meet the needs of mercantilism, so the mercantilist corporation changed to meet the needs of the expanding English economy during the first half of the nineteenth century. As industrialism progressed, the scale of enterprise enlarged and group participation in economic undertakings became increasingly desirable. The formation of medieval corporations had required a grant from the king. Later Parliament was given the right to grant corporate charters. Theoretically charters were granted only on grounds of high policy, and they spelled out in detail the limitations on the size and scope of the corporation's activities. The role of the corporation in building a liberal economy in the nineteenth century was so crucial, however, that incorporation could no longer be considered a privilege, and it became a right available to everyone. Most of the mercantilist restrictions on corporate activity were abandoned eventually.

The new circumstances required that the sovereign authority over the corporation be shifted from the crown and Parliament to the marketplace. The power inherent in corporate organization had to be kept under control so that the private interests served by the corporation would not conflict with the public interests of society. The only feasible way of doing this in a liberal economy was to depend primarily on competition to punish transgressors by causing them to fail and thus lose their power. The haziness of the distinction between public and private welfare and the dependence of the market sanction on a decentralized pattern of economic power were not clearly seen in the nineteenth century.

This brief survey suggests that the evolution of the corporation has followed a distinctive pattern. Since its inception it has had the same basic purpose of giving individuality to the actions of a group of individuals operating in concert. As the uses to which corporations have been put have progressively broadened, however, social authority over their actions has weakened. Society has allowed corporations to further private interests because at the same time they promoted the public welfare. This means that although the form of the corporation is stable, its function is not. At any one time the area of activity allowed corporations will reflect the social consensus on what private interests are sufficiently compatible with the public welfare to be permitted.

There is ample historical evidence to support the idea that the status of the corporation shifts according to the needs of society. When the economic need is uppermost, the corporation occupies a predominantly economic status and most of its activities are economic in nature. But the corporation is never entirely an economic entity, and at times the noneconomic aspects of its status and role are so important as to over-shadow the economic aspects.

The imperative drive toward industrialization in the nineteenth century focused attention on the economic elements of the corporation's status, but today the latent noneconomic aspects of its status are coming to the fore. This seems foreign to us because we are now used to the idea that we live in a society in which the division of labor has been carried out to a point where we have a high degree of structural differentiation among social institutions. We are fond of pointing out that the tribe of the primitive society has become differentiated into the institutions of the family, law, government, religion, and economy in modern industrial society. The truth is, however, that the corporation has become a less specialized entity because it alone can perform the variety of functions required to balance our material and idealistic values and goals. When this is perceived, it becomes clear that there is no reason to be anxious because the status of the corporation is in a somewhat fluid state, becoming more specialized or more general according to the shifting needs of society that can be met by the corporate form.

Economic and Noneconomic Functions of the Corporation

The function of an entity is the natural, proper, and characteristic action which it performs in the service of some larger body of which it is a part. For example, the function of gasoline in automobiles is to provide the fuel which the motor transforms into motive power. The corporation has many different functions, depending upon the frame of reference from which it is viewed. From the viewpoint of the stockholder, the corporation's function is to earn profit; from that of the worker, to provide him with a job; from the consumer's viewpoint, to supply goods of the desired price and quality. The frames of reference from which the functions of the corporation are viewed in this chapter are those of the economy and society. From these viewpoints all the functions of the corporation fall into two categories: its economic and noneconomic functions.

Economics is the study of human behavior in the allocation of scarce resources among unlimited wants. Every society has an economic system which provides its members with food, clothing, shelter, and other goods and services. There are three basic questions which must be answered by the economic system: (1) Which goods will be produced from the scarce resources? (2) how will the goods be produced? and (3) who will consume the goods? In the American economy, answers to these questions are supplied largely by the corporation. It determines which goods to produce to meet consumer demand and when, where, and how they will be produced. The corporation also has an influence on who consumes the finished product because the incomes with which consumers buy goods are largely derived from the payment of wages, dividends, and interest by the corporation. All these activities make up the economic function of the corporation. They are the natural, proper, and characteristic ways in which the corporation functions to meet the economic needs of the members of society.

Clearly the primary function of the corporation is the economic one of producing goods and services. The corporation has been developed as the key economic unit in our industrial economy because it meets the technical requirements inherent in the mass production process better than any other form of business enterprise. It has evolved to its present dominant position because the members of society have recognized the legitimacy of its economic function. On the other hand, the corporation performs political, welfare, social, and cultural functions that are non-economic in nature. These functions have not developed because of the conscious motivations of the members of society. Many citizens are not even aware that the corporation performs them. Therefore, these functions are latent in the sense that they have objective consequences for society which are not always recognized or intended. Thus the corporation's non-economic functions are of a secondary nature, and their legitimacy is not as firmly established as its economic function.

Post-World War II Expansion of Noneconomic Functions

It is highly unlikely that a modern large corporation would ever perform only economic functions or that its noneconomic functions would ever become more important than its economic function. A social organization can hardly avoid performing some secondary functions that on the surface have little or no relationship to its primary function. On the other hand, organizations are established and allowed to exist because of the recognition by the members of society that they meet a definite social need. The balance that exists at any moment of time between the primary and secondary functions performed by an organization is the result of the relationship it has with society, the social circumstances in which the organization operates, and the awareness by the members of society of the secondary functions of the organization. In the case of the corporation, all these factors have led to an expansion of secondary noneconomic functions in the post-World War II period.

Changes which occurred in the corporation and in society during the twentieth century and changes in the way in which the corporation relates to society are the major causes of the trend toward secondary noneconomic functions of the corporation. The changes which have occurred in the corporation have transformed its structure and method of operation. The most notable of these changes were the rise of big business, bureaucratization of the corporation, separation of ownership and control, professionalization of management, and the diffusion of corporate property rights.

At the same time that these changes were occurring, other important changes were taking place in the social environment of the corporation. The organizational revolution was well underway; the moral code of capitalism was being transformed; and the economic role of government was expanding.

These changes combined to produce a new relationship between the corporation and society. Instead of being a single-purpose economic organization responsible only for the production of goods and services, the corporation took on significance as a social institution in its own right. It was thrust into the forefront of social, political, and cultural life. This development has been facilitated by the increasing autonomy of the large corporation because of the relaxation of traditional market controls over business. Many managers, freed from the direct control of stockholders and no longer under the compulsion to maximize profits, have come increasingly under the influence of the idea that they are expected to conduct the affairs of the corporation in a socially responsible manner. The result of these forces has been an expansion of the public role of the corporation, and it is in fulfilling this role that the corporation has taken on noneconomic functions.

The second cause of the postwar trend toward expansion of the secondary noneconomic functions of the corporation was a shift in the circumstances in which the corporation functions. Other things being equal, an organization has greater scope for performing secondary functions when it can execute its primary function smoothly, efficiently, and with some reserve of functional capacity. During the depressed 1930s, most corporations were unable to function at a peak level in the production of goods and services because of inadequate demand. Managers had neither time nor inclination to concern themselves with anything but the survival of the enterprise. There was not the opportunity for the corporation to take on noneconomic functions because of the abnormal and dangerous circumstances in which its economic function was carried on. An almost opposite set of circumstances prevailed during World War II. Then the problem was inadequate productive capacity and shortages of labor and materials. The dependence of the war effort on a high level of production gave such a priority to the primary economic function of the corporation that its secondary noneconomic functions were deemphasized for the duration of the war.

It has been in the affluent years following World War II that the trend toward secondary noneconomic corporate functions has accelerated. Large corporations have operated during most of this period at a fairly high level of capacity utilization, and on the whole they have had a favorable profit experience. They have been able to perform their primary economic function satisfactorily with respect to the national interest and their own welfare. At the same time, they have grown and become stronger financially, so that their capacity to perform social functions has expanded. Furthermore, there has been an increasing demand by the public that corporations be more socially responsible and behave in ways that are considered beneficial to the community. The result is a tendency—which is not clearly recognized by many of the top managers who actually have implemented it—for the corporation to perform secondary noneconomic functions to a greater extent than ever before.

There usually is a lag between the time when a social institution or organization undertakes secondary social functions and the time when this is generally recognized. This has occurred in the case of the corporation. The trend toward noneconomic corporate functions has been underway for over half a century, but it has only been in the past decade or so that many students of business and society have become aware of what was happening. Thus, to some extent, the concern that currently is felt about this trend is due to a rather sudden awareness of the significance of certain corporate behavioral patterns rather than to an acceleration in the trend itself.

Social Significance of Corporate Functions

Capitalism developed in the eighteenth and nineteenth centuries as the leading way to organize industrial society. The classical economists led by Adam Smith developed a theory of capitalism as the capitalistic system triumphed in one country after another. The primary unit of analysis in the theory is the individual. He is viewed as a reasoning being who is primarily motivated by a desire to maximize his individual welfare. Competitive markets are used to spur businessmen to greater efficiency and also to dispense a stern but equitable justice to investors, workers, and resource owners. Reliance is placed on regulated self-interest to maintain social order. There is no elite which runs the capitalistic system, according to the theory, because one is not needed. The invisible hand of the competitive market assures attainment of social goals and group welfare. Organizations which concentrate power, particularly economic and political organizations, are viewed with suspicion. This theory has been an interpretation of the open society, to which the Western world has been dedicated for a century and a half.

Fascism, socialism, and communism have developed in the twentieth century as ways to organize industrial society that are alternatives to capitalism. They differ in certain respects, but all three emphasize the state as the basic social and economic unit rather than the individual. Fascism is the totalitarian organization of government, economy, and society by a single-party dictatorship which is militarist, nationalist, and imperialist. It has virtually disappeared as a worldwide movement with the defeats of Germany, Italy, and Japan in World War II. During its period of greatest vigor, it professed to offer a novel method of organizing economic relationships in autonomous corporations that were the administrative agencies of their industries. But in point of fact, the fascist corporations were merely part of the economic apparatus of the state, and they were used to coerce individuals and suppress the free interplay of the competitive open society.

Socialism has been adopted in considerable degree in countries like England and Sweden which have mixed economies. Social economic planning, which has come to be the basic principle of socialism, seems capable of operating side by side with a largely capitalistic market system.

Communism, of course, is the leading adversary of capitalism today. The Russians have demonstrated that a communistic economy can operate at a high level of output and growth. Many of the underdeveloped nations in the world are attracted to communism rather than capitalism because they have neither the political system nor the values which are essential to make capitalism work, whereas they do have the strong central government which is the essential characteristic of communism as it is found in the world today.

The question of corporate functions should be viewed from the standpoint of how to organize industrial society, if its significance is to be fully appreciated. The trend toward secondary functions of the corporation is a movement away from the purely capitalistic system. It involves the basic economic unit of the nation in the performance of noneconomic and hence nonmarket activities. Therefore, it is part of the "politicization" of economic life which substitutes political for market criteria in making economic decisions. This suggests that to the extent corporations move from economic to noneconomic functions, they are undermining capitalism. A different interpretation is possible, however. No nation any longer has a purely capitalistic system. The United States has discarded *laissez faire* and now has a system of controlled capitalism. A credible explanation of this shift is that it occurred because of the necessity of adapting capitalism to the changing conditions of the world in which we now must live. Without such adaption we might have run the risk of complete overthrowal of capitalism because of the inflexibility in meeting new and changing conditions.

Therefore, it is not self-evident whether the trend toward secondary noneconomic corporate functions is a forerunner of the development of a new type of noncapitalistic economic system or whether it is a prudent step necessary to preserve the best features of capitalism. All that we can be sure of is that the question of which functions are legitimate for the corporation to perform is fundamentally related to the larger issue of how America is to organize its economy and society in order to meet the technical requirements of industrialism and yet retain its traditional values of freedom and democracy.

The question of which functions the corporation should perform is probably not one which is salient in the thinking of the general public at this time. It may not be long, however, before it becomes one of the most hotly debated issues of the day. Americans are vitally concerned about the directions their society and way of life are taking. The gap between the American ideal of the morally, politically, and economically free individual, which is a legacy of an eighteenth-century rural and agrarian society, and the twentieth-century urban and industrial reality of the puny individual in a world of powerful and impersonal organizations is not pleasing to many Americans. They are becoming increasingly sensitive about the spiritual concessions which they believe must be made in order to attain a more abundant material life. Whether the corporation should perform secondary noneconomic functions and, if so, which ones it should perform are questions which clearly have significance for them because the answers will determine to a large extent the nature of the American Way in the industrial society of the future. When this issue becomes imperative to the average American, there likely will be a great deal of ambivalence and soul-searching before any public consensus develops.

Functional Problems of Society

Enough has been said about this matter of corporate functions to indicate that it is an important and complex one. People often take very strong positions about it, positions which are highly ideological in the sense that they are emotionally charged and have little of the objectivity of science. It is understandable that this is the case, because the issue of corporate functions has a bearing on many of our most cherished values and goals. Is not this all the more reason to approach this question as scientifically as possible? What is needed is a theory of the functions of the corporation which will enable us to tell which corporate functions are legitimate and which are not.

Sociologists tend to agree that survival is the most fundamental goal of society, and in order to survive it must solve four functional problems: (1) goal attainment, (2) adaption, (3) integration, and (4) pattern maintenance and tension management.[1] The problem of goal attainment arises from the need to coordinate the members of society in cooperative endeavors. Society is organized in accordance with the principle of the division of labor. Each member of society specializes in the performance of a particular task. Their efforts must be meshed together and organized into a coherent and cooperative whole. Cooperation implies an attitude toward coordination, which can be thought of as the formal regulation of interdependent specialists to attain common goals. Thus goal attainment involves solving the problem of coordination needed to keep society moving steadily toward whatever goals it has.

Closely related to the goal attainment problem of society is that of adaption. The adaptive problem concerns the way in which society transforms its human and nonhuman resources for the purpose of attaining its goals. Adaption is basically concerned with economizing—the allocating of a given stock of scarce resources among different ends so as to achieve as much satisfaction as possible. Economizing involves the twin social processes of rational calculation and control. To be rational is to select among alternative means the ones most likely to achieve the desired end. To be rationally calculating in meeting the functional problem of adaption is to calculate the advantages and disadvantages of different ways of using resources and to select the combination which results in the highest level of attainment of the goals of society. Control involves having power over the actions of others. Since many individuals perform different but related adaptive activities, control must be exercised to co-ordinate their efforts so as to avoid conflicts and to obtain the best results.

Integration is the process of creating harmony in society. To some extent, the members of society must be loyal to one another and to the social system as a whole. This is necessary because a low level of integration would endanger the society by undermining the basis of cooperation among its members. Strains and conflicts develop in society because of the processes of goal attainment and adaption. One source of such difficulties is the sharing of rewards. Each member of society must be rewarded for his contribution toward attainment of social goals, There may develop competition over such rewards, which are scarce, even though they are the fruits of cooperation. An example is conflict between labor and management over the division of business income. Such a conflict must be kept in bounds if society is to maintain the degree of cohesion it needs to survive and function effectively.

Pattern maintenance and tension management also are concerned with maintaining the equilibrium of society. But whereas the functional problem of integration deals with the relationship among members of society, pattern maintenance and tension management focus on the individual members of society. If society is to preserve itself, it must ward off external threats and challenges to its value system and to the cultural patterns based on values. The members of society must learn these values and culture patterns and have an attitude of respect toward them. From time to time they must be renewed, so to speak, through appropriate rituals and other symbols. It is particularly important for the maintenance of society that its members continue to regard societal goals as legitimate. It is the function of pattern maintenance to protect and promote social values and culture patterns.

Tension management deals with the problem of the emotional disturbances and distractions of the members of society. These must be "managed" if individuals are to carry on effectively. It is important that they be relatively well satisfied with the rewards they get for helping to attain societal goals. Tension management has the task of keeping members of society sufficiently gratified so that they can perform their tasks properly. If they become frustrated because they feel they are not being properly rewarded in money, prestige, and other sources of gratification, tension may mount to the point where their efficiency is seriously impaired.

Functional Subsystems of Society

Every society develops a functional subsystem to deal with each of the four functional problems described above. Any individual, social system, organization, or social institution which contributes to the way in which society meets one of its functional problems is a part of the functional subsystem that develops in society to cope with that particular problem.

Government is the social institution most directly concerned with the functional problem of goal attainment. It is through governmental processes that society determines which goals to pursue and which means to use in attaining them. Government is the main center of power and control in society. It is necessary that some members of society have the power necessary to force individuals to cooperate in attaining system-wide goals, and those with the broadest power over people are members of government (e.g., the President, Supreme Court justices, congressmen). On the other hand, there are other individuals in society who exercise power and are not members of government. Generals, ministers, business managers, educators, advertisers, and propagandists have power and use it to influence the goals of society and the means to attain them. This also is true of organizations, such as political parties, churches, labor unions, and trade associations. All of these individuals and organizations are part of the goal attainment subsystem of society because in their activities they mobilize the power needed by society to attain its collective goals.

Just as government plays the central role in the goal attainment subsystem, so the economy has the primary responsibility for the adaptive subsystem. The basic adaptive problem—to adapt human and nonhuman resources so that they satisfy human wants and needs—is solved by economic activity. But the economy is not the only social institution which serves adaptive functions. The government in its defense programs is performing an adaptive function by transforming resources into the form required for national security. The schools also perform an adaptive function by upgrading the human resources of society into a generalized facility to be used in pursuit of many social goals. An educated populace is more effective in producing goods and services in peacetime and in fighting in wartime.

The family plays the primary role in pattern maintenance and tension management. It is the main agency of socialization in society. As children we learn in the family the acceptable patterns of behavior and the code of our society. We learn to respect and identify with the basic cultural patterns and social goals of society to such a degree that we are unable, in good conscience, to think and act much differently. The family also plays a part in the day-to-day management of tension. The home is a place of sanctuary for the individual where he can be himself and release the tensions stored up in his interactions during the day in the outside world. Other groups make up the pattern maintenance and tension management subsystem besides the family. Schools, religious groups, and recreational groups bear responsibility for pattern maintenance; and hospitals and other health organizations, as well as recreational and religious groups, play a part in tension management.

The integrative subsystem is not as closely identified with a particular social institution as the other three functional subsystems. Any social institution or agency which functions to achieve solidarity among the members of society is part of the integrative subsystem. Examples in our society are law, police, social workers, journalism, religion, and psychiatry. These agencies and institutions function to "bring into line" the behavior of the individual members and groups in accordance with the integrative needs of society. They check or reverse tendencies to deviant behavior, and they promote the conditions of harmonious cooperation.

Functions of the Corporation in the Functional Subsystems

The discussion of the functional problems and functional subsystems of society offers a basis for classifying and analyzing the functions of the corporation. As we have seen, any individual, social system, organization, or social institution which contributes to the way in which society meets one of its functional problems is a part of the functional subsystem which deals with that particular problem. These social entities are not so highly specialized in function that they contribute to solving only one of the functional problems of society. The corporation is such a central organization in modern industrial society that it plays a role in all four functional subsystems. Thus the primary economic and secondary non-economic functions of the corporation can be classified according to the problems with which they deal and the functional subsystems in which they are performed.

The corporation performs its primary economic function in the adaptive subsystem of society. Despite the trend toward secondary noneconomic functions, the prime function of the corporation has been, and continues to be, the production of wealth. Its functions in the other three functional subsystems are secondary in the sense that the corporation could continue to exist without performing them. Without the capacity to produce goods and services, however, the corporation undoubtedly would disappear. This does not mean, however, that the only function which the corporation performs in the adaptive subsystem is the production of goods and services. The gifts which corporations make to private colleges and universities can be viewed within this framework. As we have seen, education belongs in the adaptive subsystem because it is an important means of adapting human resources so that they can better attain the goals of society. Thus by helping to finance private education the corporation contributes to the overall adaptability of society.

The corporation necessarily performs a function in the goal attainment subsystem because of the power which is vested in it. Before the rise of big business, it was thought that the ownership of the enterprise by the entrepreneur took it out of political control. But the separation of ownership and control in the large corporation has added a political dimension to business. The modern corporate manager acts more like a political officeholder than an entrepreneur. He is responsible to several constituencies: owners, workers, suppliers, dealers, customers, government, and the local community. He uses the power he exercises in the corporation's name to balance the interests of all these constituencies. This diffuseness of corporate goals, compared to the older rule of profit maximization, has led to an overlapping of private and public activities. Thus the corporation is not merely an instrument to be used by government in attaining the goals of society. It functions itself as a coordinator to achieve broad social goals.

The corporation performs several different functions in the integrative subsystem of society. In a pluralistic society, a certain amount of conflict between economic interest groups is expected and sanctioned. But it must not get out of hand or the continuity of the system will be threatened. The corporation is the battleground where these battles are fought. The industrial jurisprudence which is developing within the corporation as a result of modern arbitration procedures helps to prevent economic breakdown because of dissatisfaction by economic groups. Also important in this regard is the balancing-of-interests function of the manager. By meeting the needs and demands of each group tolerably well, management helps to prevent the kind of class conflict that Marx predicted would be the undoing of capitalism. A second aspect of the integrative function of the corporation is its marketing activities. From the viewpoint of the enterprise, advertising, product innovation, and sales promotion are means of nonprice competition. But from the social viewpoint they serve to keep at a high pitch the consumer orientation in American life. If consumption lags behind production, investment will fall off; and this will have a dampening effect on the entire economy. Corporate marketing activities which motivate the broad mass of consumers to continually desire a higher standard of living thus help to integrate supply and demand. Finally, corporations in recent years have made some contribution toward achieving racial integration through instituting nondiscriminatory hiring policies and tending not to locate in towns and cities where racial disputes break out frequently.

The phenomenon of the human relations movement in American industry can be interpreted in terms of the corporation's function in the pattern maintenance and tension management functional subsystem. Workers and managers, like other Americans, want all of the individuality, freedom, democracy, and equality that they believe existed in an earlier America. Such a yearning stems from an idealized image of the agrarian past and can only be disappointed in our modern bureaucratic industrial system. If the gap between our spiritual and material values and goals becomes too apparent, the legitimacy of one or both of them will come into question. The industrial human relations program which corporations organize (whatever their other functions may be) serves the function of relieving the tension between the ideal and reality of the economic aspects of American life.

Legitimacy of Corporate Functions

The analysis of the functional problems and functional subsystems of society offers a framework for analyzing and classifying the functions of the corporation, but it does not offer a basis for asserting which functions the corporation ought to perform. Simply because the corporation presently performs a particular function does not mean that it should be doing so. What is needed is a method of determining which functions the corporation legitimately should perform. This is basically an ethical question. Peter Drucker has pointed out that in "the pursuit of its everyday 'private business,' and in performing its economic job, big business is expected to further human values, and to serve national purpose."[2] The question of the legitimacy of corporate functions concerns which of all the organizational functions which further human values and serve the national purpose should be performed by the corporation.

The general concept of "legitimacy" deals with the rightness of the actions and activities of individuals, groups, and organizations. "The test of 'rightness' may be rather conscious, articulated, logically structured norms (such as a theory of the appropriate role of judicial review in a democratic order). Or the test may be the less conscious, more incoherent norms with less logical structure and abstract theory, the 'feeling' of what is right and wrong in a given instance."[3] Thus the ultimate sources of legitimacy are our social attitudes, beliefs, and values. For something to be legitimate, it must be considered compatible with, and a manifestation of, the American value system. To determine the legitimacy of corporate functions, therefore, it is necessary to understand the American value system and how the functioning of the corporation is related to it.

Values are the criteria by which individuals choose goals. They concern the things in which people are interested—things they want, desire to become, feel as obligatory, worship, and enjoy. Robin Williams defines values as *modes of organizing conduct*—meaningful, affectively invested pattern principles that guide human actions."[4] Social values are values which are shared by a majority of the members of society and considered by them to be matters of collective welfare for the entire social system.

There are two main categories of social value in American life: (1) an idealistic set of values based on ideas about the relations which should exist between individuals and between the individual and the state and (2) a materialistic set of values which emphasizes work, practicality, achievement, and the comforts of life. These two types of values show up in every attempt to analyze the American value system. For example, Williams lists the following values as dominant in American society: achievement, success, activity, work, a moral orientation, humanitarianism, efficiency, practicality, progress, material comfort, equality, freedom, science, democracy, and individual personality.[5]

Clearly the function of producing goods and services is an important activity in a society which has such a strong materialistic element in its value system. This is the source of the legitimacy of the primary economic function of the corporation. The source of legitimacy of the secondary noneconomic corporate functions is not so obvious. To get at this relationship it is necessary to consider the collectivization of political, economic, and social life which has been referred to earlier as the "organizational revolution."

The ideological issue of capitalism versus communism largely concerns the role to be played by the various organizations in the industrialized organizational society. So far the leading organizations to emerge are the corporation and the national government. Only they have the power, resources, administrative organization, and geographical scope to minister to the new and urgent needs of the organizational society. But what of the relationship between them—which will dominate the other? In every society one social institution—government, economy, religion, education, or the family—plays the central role in unifying the social system; and it dominates the others. The pattern is clear in the case of Russia. Government is the dominant social institution, and the economy is in a subordinate position. But historically the economy has been the dominant social institution in America. It is only in this century that its position has been challenged by government (the number of employees in the executive branch increased from 230,000 in 1900 to 2,355,000 in 1959).

We are living in an age in which there is an uneasy dualism between the national government and the large corporation. Each overlaps the other in terms of the functions it performs. Government intervenes in the economy in a thousand ways, and the corporation performs many functions that are essentially public in nature. There has been a merging of public and private which has blurred the clear line of demarcation that previously could be drawn between the large private corporation and public agencies. As is the case with all dualisms of this sort, however, one of the parties eventually will emerge as supreme. Thus the modern state triumphed over the Catholic Church after 1,000 years of uneasy coexistence and became the main unifying agency of society in the post-medieval world.

At this time, however, the issue in the United States remains in doubt. Because of our strong belief in freedom and democracy and our mistrust of concentrated political power, we have placed various restraints on government. Wherever possible, we rely on nongovernment sources of co-ordination. This basically is the source of legitimacy of the secondary noneconomic functions of the corporation. We recognize the need for social functions to be performed by large and powerful organizations. When faced with a choice between government and the corporation in the performance of such functions, we prefer the corporation if the function can be related in any meaningful way to its primary economic function. Big business is viewed with suspicion by many Americans because it represents such a massive concentration of power; but it is less suspect than government because the business power is in private hands and there are many separate corporations which compete to some degree, whereas there is only one monolithic Federal government.

At this time it is impossible to say which of the secondary noneconomic functions of the corporation will prove to be legitimate in the long run. It is too early to know the nature of the equilibrium relationship that will develop between government and the corporation in the organizational society. It appears highly unlikely, however, that government will ever dominate the corporation in America as it does in Russia. For this to happen, we would have to turn our backs on some of our most fundamental values. The corporation will undoubtedly continue to perform a number of noneconomic functions, and when the social role of the corporation is more clearly perceived, they will be considered legitimate. Therefore, the economists, political scientists, jurists, and businessmen who criticize the corporation for performing noneconomic functions will find that, as time goes by, their arguments will fall on increasingly deaf ears.

Evolving Status of the Manager

Evolution of the status of the manager has gone hand in hand with evolution in the status of the corporation. The concept of structural differentiation, first introduced in Chapter 3, is helpful in understanding how the manager's status has evolved. The process of structural differentiation is a general explanation of structural change. When changing circumstances render an existing structural entity inefficient because it is too generalized to function effectively in the new situation, the structure breaks up into two or more of its constituent parts. Each part now has an independent existence and specializes in the performance of part of the functions of the old structure. Taken together, the new structural entities are the functional equivalent of the old structure. They function more effectively, however, because of the greater specialization of labor that structural differentiation has made possible.

An example of the process of structural differentiation is provided by the historical evolution of marketing institutions. When distribution was in an early stage of development, there was no distinction between wholesaling and retailing, and they were carried on simultaneously in the same enterprise. But as the market expanded and there were increasing opportunities for specialization of marketing functions, the existing institutional arrangement became unwieldy. Through the process of structural differentiation, separate wholesale and retail institutions developed. As the market continued to expand, further structural differentiation occurred and more specialized kinds of wholesaling establishments and retailing establishments came into being.

The process of structural differentiation also occurs in the professions. The earliest doctors were all general practitioners. But the expansion of the market for medical services and the increase in medical knowledge have led to the development of the many specialties of modern medical practice. The same thing has occurred in the practice of law and the practice of business management. The structural differentiation of the practice of business management can be demonstrated by contrasting the managerial functions performed by the preeminent businessmen in the stages of mercantile capitalism, industrial capitalism, and big-business capitalism.

In the period roughly between the thirteenth and eighteenth centuries, it was the merchant who occupied the center of the stage of capitalism. Indeed, without him there could not have been capitalism in that period. Production of goods took place on a small scale in geographically isolated locations, and transportation and communication facilities were rudimentary. Through the efforts of the merchant, producing and consuming areas were tied together. He financed the production of goods for export, transported the goods to markets in which they were scarce, stored them, and eventually sold them. The merchant thus performed all the major functions of business: production, finance, transporation, warehousing, and marketing.

In time technological development and improvements in transportation and communication led to a significant change in the business world. Roads were built, the compass was discovered, and the seas were charted.

Movement between the different economic areas of Western Europe became much freer. Trade increased sufficiently so that areas were able to specialize in the production of the goods and services in which they had a natural advantage. This specialization of production and the expansion of international trade were forerunners of the next stage of capitalism—industrial capitalism. With the discovery of the steam engine, it was possible to substitute inanimate sources of power for the muscles of men and animals. Inevitably there was a great wave of inventions in laborsaving machinery, and this in turn led to new forms of economic organization. The factory system and the modern corporation came into being to serve the needs of the new technology.

The old role of the merchant became too generalized and unwieldy to serve efficiently in the new industrial economic order. It was necessary to separate the merchant's basic function of marketing from his production and financial activities. Trading was still important, but production was now the dynamic segment of the economy. The process of structural differentiation led to a breaking up of the merchant role into the two related roles of the trader and the entrepreneur. The entrepreneur was now at the center of the economic process. He accumulated capital, set up a manufacturing business, and managed it himself. Whereas the merchant had functioned to tie together small and isolated trading areas, the entrepreneuer had as his mission the expansion of industrial production through the practical application of the scientific discoveries of the eighteenth and nineteenth centuries.

By means of innovations in technology and administrative organization, the entrepreneur was able to build increasingly larger economic units. The growth in the size of enterprise transformed industrial capitalism into big-business capitalism and eventually led to the demise of the entrepreneur. The giant corporation, employing thousands of workers and turning out a wide variety of goods and services, could not be actively managed by the owners. In order to finance these industrial giants, it was necessary to sell stock to thousands of individuals. The actual management of the enterprise had to be turned over to professional executives. Thus the entrepreneur became structurally differentiated into the manager and the stockholder. Previously the entrepreneur had owned and managed his own business. Now the owners became passive in management matters, although they retained legal control over the business. Professional managers who had the training, skills, and experience necessary to administer the vast industrial empires of big-business corporations were given the necessary authority to do the job.

The analysis of this study suggests that further differentiation of the manager role is underway. In a free enterprise economy, it is essential that management concern itself closely with profits. Profit is necessary for the survival of the enterprise, and the profit rate remains a useful measure of the social service rendered by the enterprise. At the same time, if managers are only concerned with profit making, it is quite possible that they will use their vast power in ways considered wrong by most Americans. The solution to this dilemma is to differentiate the manager role into two parts. One part—let us call it the operating manager role—will continue to be concerned with day-to-day operations and this type of manager will be profit-minded. The other part—let us call it the socially responsible manager role—will be concerned with questions dealing with the philosophical aspects of management (e.g., What are the proper functions of business as an institution? What role should the corporation play in the community?). In short, the socially responsible manager role will bridge the gap between the necessary detail of running a business and the well-being of the social environment in which the enterprise functions.

Functions of the Manager

The functions of the manager are derived from the functions of the corporation. In the broadest sense, the function of the manager is to direct the affairs of the corporation in such a way that it performs its functions in each of the subsystems concerned with the functional imperatives facing industrial society.

This interpretation makes possible a more definite distinction between those managers who are socially responsible and those who are not. The socially responsible manager has some insight into the broader social functions of the corporation, and he makes decisions and chooses alternative courses of action with these functions in mind. He may not consciously perceive the corporation's role in the highly abstract way in which it is presented here, but he will try to direct the corporation's affairs in the way "that society expects of me." The "tough-minded" manager who actually bases every decision on the principle of profit maximization consciously or unconsciously rejects the manager role and instead chooses to play the role of the entrepreneur. Probably the majority of managers fall between these extremes. They play the manager role in a rather haphazard way; and if they are challenged about any socially oriented action, they defend it ideologically in terms of profit maximization.

In analyzing the functions of the manager, it is necessary to distinguish between two social systems in which the manager participates. On the one hand, a manager occupies an *office* in a particular corporation. This designates "a position in a deliberately created organization, governed by specific and limited rules in a limited group, more generally achieved than ascribed."[6] This is the notion of manager that prevails in the literature dealing with organization theory and management functions. For our purposes, the manager role has an outward focus from the corporation. It designates "a position in the general institutional system, recognized and supported by the entire society, spontaneously evolved rather than deliberately created, rooted in the folkways and mores."[7]

NOTES

1 Professor Talcott Parsons of Harvard University has been a leader in analyzing the functional problems of society. For a technical review and critique of his theory, see Chandler Morse, "The Functional Imperatives," in Max Black (ed.), *The Social Theories of Talcott Parsons* (Englewood Cliffs, N.J.: Prentice-Hall, Inc., 1961).

2 Peter Drucker, "Big Business and the National Purpose," *Harvard Business Review,* vol. 40, no. 2 (March–April, 1962), p. 59.

3 Robert A. Dahl and Charles E. Lindblom, *Politics, Economics and Welfare* (New York: Harper & Row, Publishers, Incorporated, 1953), pp. 114–115.

4 Robin M. Williams, Jr., *American Society* (New York: Alfred A. Knopf, Inc., 1957), p. 375.

5 *Ibid.,* pp. 390–440.

6 Kingsley Davis, *Human Society* (New York: The Macmillan Company, 1949), pp. 88–89.

7 *Ibid.,* p. 89.

8

Making
Socially
Responsible
Decisions

The three preceding chapters suggest that in the not too distant future the ideological and theoretical support required for widespread acceptance of the doctrine and ethic of social responsibility by the public and business community will be forthcoming. Social responsibility will then become transformed from an implicit to an explicit ethic and supplant the profit ethic in ideology and theory as it already is starting to supplant it in fact. When that day comes (of course, it is already here for some leading executives), the discussion about the social responsibility of managers will become less normative and more analytical than at present. Rather than debate the existence, validity, and importance of the social responsibilities of corporate managers, the emphasis will be on how managers actually go about making socially responsible decisions. This chapter deals with that question.

Function of the Socially Responsible Manager

There are three levels in the hierarchical structure of organizations: (1) the technical level; (2) the managerial level; and (3) the social level.[1] The technical level produces the goods and services which are the organization's output. In any but the smallest organizations, there are suborganizations that function at the technical level; and they must be coordinated for productive efficiency. The coordination function is performed at the management level. There is a management system at this level which controls and services the technical system at the lower technical level. The management level in turn is controlled and serviced by the higher social level. The organization is not an autonomous social system, and it must be integrated into its social environment. This is the function of the social level of organization.

The management system has internal and external relations. Its internal relations are concerned with the technical system. Decisions made in the management system control the operations in the technical system, but managerial decisions on highly technical questions are made in consultation with technical personnel. The technical system also influences the management system by specifying the resources needed to carry out the organization's technical function. Thus one aspect of the external relations of management is the mediation between the technical system and groups in the organization's environment, some of whom provide the organization with its resources and others who take its output.

Differences in the status and role of the socially responsible manager and the operating manager show up clearly in the structural and functional analysis of the corporate organization. There is a division of labor in decision making. The socially responsible manager makes policy decisions concerning the goals of the enterprise and the major steps necessary to achieve them. The operating manager makes the allocative and integrative decisions which implement policy within the organization. The socially responsible manager services and controls the operating manager by seeing to it that he has the necessary resource inputs for corporate goal attainment and that these goals are attained properly, just as the operating manager services and controls first-line supervisors at the technical level of organization. The operating manager's focus of interest is the internal operation of the corporation whereas the socially responsible manager's orientation is outward.

The socially responsible manager's position is unique in that he is the only member of the management hierarchy who operates simultaneously in two systems of action: the corporation and society. The socially responsible manager is most clearly distinguished from operating managers by the totality of his authority and responsibility. He is the only member of management who does not report to a superior manager concerning the performance of a particular part of the corporation's operations. He occupies a position of leadership within the corporation and one of responsibility in society. He is given the key task in democratic industrial society of administering the capital, human, and natural resources of the corporation. To do this effectively, the socially responsible manager must act as a middleman between the corporation and society, interpreting one to the other and smoothing out differences in values and needs before they lead to serious conflict. In short, the basic function of the socially responsible manager is integrative. He must integrate the separate elements of the corporation into an efficient organizational entity and integrate the corporate organization into the social scheme of things.

In the outward orientation of the socially responsible manager's role, he determines which goals society wants the corporation to pursue and the balance between them. The most important decisions he makes establish the long-range policies of the corporation. These decisions are based on premises about long-term goals and the relatively permanent means to be used in attaining them. "The premises for these decisions are largely derived from predictions of the set of social and economic conditions in which the company will be living during the next few years. These environmental conditions, in the main, will be determined by the goals, means and premises of certain groups of people *outside* the company—by what they will be thinking and doing."[2] Therefore, the socially responsible manager must be able to anticipate the responses to long-range goals and the means to attain them of the individuals and groups who are beyond the corporation's immediate sphere of influence. Unless he can do so with a fair degree of accuracy, decisions he makes today will seem mistaken, unrealistic, and even antisocial in the years ahead.

The rise of socially responsible management has been due in large part to the inability of the board of directors to function effectively as an intermediary between the corporation and society. The board originally was conceived as the guardian of the interests of the stockholders. As the idea developed that corporate management is responsible to society as a whole, the board might have evolved into an agency for mediation between the management system of the corporate organization and the external environment. In this capacity it could have influenced management to operate the corporation in the public interest. As it is, of course, the board of directors tends in most cases to rubberstamp top management policies and decisions.

The reason for the failure of a more socially oriented line of evolution probably lies in the American proclivity for coping with problems of social change in an implicit way. For the board of directors to be set up explicitly as the organization to control the corporation in the public interest would be to publicly acknowledge that a conflict of interests does exist. This would undermine the whole belief system upon which the free enterprise system was founded. We have followed a much less disruptive approach: We have bypassed the board of directors and through the process of structural differentiation evolved a new type of manager whose major function is to prevent such a conflict of interest from developing.

The basic reason for the evolution of the role of the socially responsible manager is the need to make the corporation an adaptive entity in a highly dynamic society. For society to maintain itself, there must be a minimal level of harmony and unity of its organizations and social institutions. They must all pull in the same general direction and work together relatively smoothly. This is why organizations and social institutions are so highly interdependent. No one can go in an opposite direction from the others without seriously disrupting social equilibrium. If one were to strike out on a drastically different path than the others, the rest of society would not likely change direction and follow it. More likely the organization or institution out of phase with the others would be discarded and its function taken over by another or by a new one that would evolve. If the corporation were to take a path at odds with the rest of society, it would be eliminated and another economic entity would take over its major functions. This is the kind of long-run competition which Schumpeter had in mind when he talked of the process of creative destruction.

Philip Selznick's analysis of leadership in administration is helpful in understanding the socially responsible manager's function of ensuring the survival of the corporation. Selznick distinguishes between organizations and institutions: An organization "refers to an *expendable tool*, a rational instrument engineered to do a job," whereas an institution "is more nearly a natural product of social needs and pressures—a responsive, adaptive organism."[3] Institutionalization is a process which over time turns an organization into an institution. When this has occurred, the organization is so identified with broad social values and goals that it is no longer considered expendable. The most significant meaning of institutionalization is "*to infuse with value* beyond the technical requirements of the task at hand."[4] Thus a basic function of socially responsible managers collectively is to facilitate the infusion of social values into corporations so as to transform the corporate form from an organization into an institution and further its survival in a dynamic world. The socially responsible manager, like Selznick's institutional leader, "*is primarily an expert in the promotion and protection of values.*"[5]

Means and Ends in Business Decision Making

Now let us look at how managers go about making socially responsible decisions. First, there is the matter of the factual and ethical content of business decisions. Every decision contains a factual element in the sense that it implies a set of factual consequences. For example, a management decision to introduce a new product might be based on the following line of reasoning: The new product will increase sales, expand the firm's share of the market, lead to larger profits, and result in greater stockholder dividends. These consequences of the decision are factual in the sense that they are susceptible to empirical proof. "In principle, factual propositions may be tested to determine whether they are *true* or *false*—whether what they say about the world actually occurs, or whether it does not."[6] Either sales increase or they do not; the corporation's market share expands or it does not; and profits and dividends go up or they do not.

Decisions also contain an ethical element. When management is in a decision-making situation, there generally are many different alternatives that might be selected. Each one leads to a particular stream of events in the future. Thus when management makes a decision, in effect it selects one state of anticipated affairs in preference to others. Whether or not this outcome is better than any of the other possible alternatives is a matter of ethical judgment rather than of fact.

For example, suppose management has decided to introduce a new product and now must decide which of two different items to bring out. The first has the potential to greatly increase sales, substantially expand the firm's share of its most important market, and greatly enhance the corporate image with the public. But heavy research and development outlays and advertising and promotional expenditures will be required to successfully introduce this product, and the net addition to corporate profits that it can be expected to produce in the short run will be slight. The second product will develop a new market rapidly, have a relatively slight impact on the corporate image, and produce a larger net profit than the first one. One cannot decide which of the two products to introduce without making an ethical judgment. To say that one outcome is better than the other is to say "what ought to be," and this is a subjective ethical matter rather than an objective factual one.

The source of the ethical element in business decisions is the objective of the enterprise. Business decisions are purposive—they are intended to lead to the attainment of certain desired ends by organizing and manipulating available means. Each decision is at the same time a means and an end. In our example the new product to be introduced is a means to the end of increased sales. But increased sales is itself the means to the end of greater profit, and the latter is a means to the end of more dividends. Thus there is a hierarchy of means and ends in business decision making. At the source of this hierarchy is the objective of the enterprise, the reason for which it was founded and/or continues to exist.

All business decisions play a part in the means-ends network which develops to achieve this objective.

Traditionally profit maximization has been considered the objective of business. This viewpoint has the great advantages, from the standpoint of the ethics of decision making, of clarity and certainty. The businessman is never in doubt about what he is trying to accomplish. Price and output are set at the levels where marginal revenue equals marginal cost. All decisions are made on the basis of their impact on profits. The businessman need not consider any values or goals that cannot be expressed in money terms and which do not affect the profit position of the enterprise. Therefore, the businessman can operate on a completely rational and objective basis. He need not take into account subjective and psychological phenomena in making decisions.

The doctrine of socially responsible management complicates the decision-making process. If management is responsible to several groups in society, this means that the enterprise will have multiple objectives which reflect the goals, values, and ends of these groups. Clearly there will be conflicts among these goals (e.g., customers desire lower prices, employees want higher wages, and stockholders want greater dividends). Such conflicts complicate the decision-making process because now management is faced with several alternative means-ends hierarchies, depending upon which objective is considered most urgent, instead of a single means-ends hierarchy, as in the profit-maximization case. Therefore, the ethical component of decision making is tremendously enlarged in scope. When profit is the objective of decision making, management has a clear picture of ends; and it is factually oriented because its major problem is to select the best means to the end of profit maximization. But when social responsibility is the objective of decision making, management must determine the best combination of ends as well as the best means to those ends. It must take into account a wide range of value phenomena in deciding on ends, phenomena which are inherently highly subjective and psychological in nature.

Suppose a decision must be made whether or not to move a branch plant from a small town in which it is the economic mainstay to another area where production costs are lower. Whichever decision is made will have differential effects on the various groups involved. If the move is made and production costs are appreciably lower, profits may go up and lead to higher stockholder dividends; hourly earnings of workers may go up because of increased productivity; and customers may get a better product, a lower price, or both. On the other hand, the small town may become economically stagnant, and workers who are well settled in the town may face the choice of dislocation (and perhaps a cut in wages) or loss of job.

If profit is the sole objective of decision making, profit is the only relevant value to take into account in making the decision. The impact of moving or not moving the plant on worker, customer, and community is significant only insofar as it affects profits. But if social responsibility is the objective of decision making, a host of other values are relevant (e.g., achievement, success, humanitarianism, efficiency, practicality, progress, equality, freedom). Furthermore, there will be conflicts between these values. The move may further practicality and efficiency, but it may be opposed on humanitarian grounds. In order to make a socially responsible decision, it is necessary to determine which values are involved and decide what priority they should have where they are in conflict.

Decision Making under Conditions of Value Conflict

One way of dealing with the problem of decision making under conditions of conflicting values is to follow the practice which some philosophers advocate of basing conduct in specific situations on general values. The philosopher sets aside the particular situation calling for decision and asks what he would prefer in all situations in which the same set of values is found. Thus he seeks to determine a permanent and universal ranking of values. Once such a ranking is established, he determines which of his immediate alternatives in the situation calling for decision is consistent with this general value order. "He has looked away from his own conflict of the moment and decided what in general is most worthwhile."[7]

There are four steps in this approach:

1 Identify the values involved in the situation.
2 Rank the values.
3 Identify the possible alternative decisions.
4 Select the decision which is consistent with the general value ranking.

The value-ranking approach has the advantages of simplicity and practicality, but it suffers from a conceptual difficulty: It gives no indication of which decision is best when the choice is between alternatives offering different combinations of benefits. The best decision is not necessarily the one which maximizes the leading value because it may go against values lower on the list which collectively are more important than the top value. If there are five values involved in a decision-making situation—V1, V2, V3, V4, V5—it is not clear whether a decision favoring V1 and V4 is superior to one favoring V2, V3, and V5. The value-ranking approach does not even indicate whether a decision favoring V1 alone is better than one favoring V2, because the quantitative factor is missing. A decision which favors V1 by 2 units of utility and V2 by 50 units is probably preferable to one which favors V1 by 5 units and V2 by 3 units.

A way of avoiding this problem is provided by the rational-deductive approach, an application to the field of values of the deductive type of thinking characteristic of science. This approach was first conceived by Plato, and it has influenced ethical thought ever since. It overcomes the conceptual difficulty of choosing when the choice is between alternatives offering different combinations of benefits by setting up a system of principles and intermediate principles from which decisions can be logically deduced in particular situations.

There are four steps to this approach:

1 State ultimate values in the form of general principles as precisely as possible.
2 State the conditions under which each principle governs the application of the others.
3 Derive intermediate principles suitable for application in particular situations.
4 Get the facts in the particular situation and logically deduce the decision.

For example, suppose an individual's value system could be expressed in terms of the following general principles: (1) Always behave in an honorable way; (2) the family comes first; and (3) never borrow needlessly. A series of intermediate principles could be derived from these general principles: (1) When a family member is in serious danger, everything possible must be done to protect him or her; (2) luxuries must be paid for out of savings or current income; and so on. Let us say this individual must make a decision whether or not to steal from his employer. To deduce the right decision, all he need do is gather the information required by the intermediate principles. If his wife desperately needed an operation and there were no other sources of money available, he would steal. If his wife wanted a new car to impress the neighbors, he would not.

Welfare economics also deals with the problem of making decisions when competing values are involved. This field is concerned with defining the conditions under which the allocation of resources would maximize the satisfaction of consumer wants. To achieve such an optimum, a number of decisions must be made simultaneously concerning production, consumption, savings, and investment. Economists have pondered over whether values or ends should have any influence on these decisions.

Kenneth Arrow accepts the necessity of dealing with conflicting values on decisions about resource allocation, but he does not believe it is necessary to explicitly stipulate these values. He argues that all that is required is to be able to decide between various possible states of affairs in society. To make a decision between two or more different social states, it is not necessary to make deductions from formulated principles. A decision can be made simply by taking into account all the features of each state of society that are subject to preference.

Arrow has stated the position in this way: "As with any type of behavior described by maximization, the measurability of social welfare need not be assumed; all that matters is the existence of a social ordering . . . all that is needed to define such an ordering is to know the relative ranking of each pair of alternatives."[8] This means the decision maker need not explicitly formulate his values and organize them in order of priority. Therefore, all the unconscious psychological mechanisms which influence value judgments are allowed to operate freely. One can make a decision by selecting the alternative which subjectively seems superior without rationalizing the basis of his decision.

Braybrooke and Lindblom have outlined a new strategy of decision making, called disjointed incrementalism, which also deals with conflicting values. They reason that the decision maker starts with a knowledge of present conditions and objectives. He gains more information in order to get a clearer picture of the status quo. Then he compares alternatives which are similar but distinguishably different from the present situation. He is "concerned with margins at which it is contemplated that social states might be changed from that existing . . . he concentrates his evaluations on what we call margins or increments, that is, on the increments by which value ouputs or value consequences differ."[9]

One advantage of the incremental approach to decision making is that the decision maker simplifies his problem by concentrating on ameliorating social evils rather than attaining utopias.[10] He may have a hard time visualizing which of the possible decisions would lead to the best of all possible worlds, but generally he knows what his most pressing problems are and which decision would do the most to alleviate them.

The New Morality of situation ethics, which is advocated by many liberal Protestant clergymen and theologians, is yet another approach to the problem of making decisions under conditions of value conflict. This view of Christian morality is opposed to the legalism of the traditional point of view. Traditionally, universal principles of right and wrong are thought to be derived from God and to come down to earth directly from heaven. They are considered eternally valid for human conduct. Certain forms of behavior are always wrong and nothing can make them right. There can be no question about Christian standards, according to this view; the only question is whether men live up to them. This approach to morality has wide popular appeal. It has the kind of absoluteness and certainty that men expect the church to stand for in a world of change and doubt.

There are two key propositions to the New Morality of situation ethics: (1) Love is the only ethic which has any fixity in a world of change and yet is adaptable to the changing scene; (2) nothing can of itself always be labeled wrong. One cannot say that premarital sex relations, divorce, or even murder are wrong or sinful in themselves, because the only intrinsic evil is lack of love. People matter, and their welfare is affected by the situations in which they find themselves. The deepest welfare of particular people in particular situations matters more than anything in the world. What is in their best interests is a matter of love, not standards. As Paul Tillich said, "The absoluteness of love is its power to go into the concrete situation, to discover what is demanded by the predicament of the concrete to which it turns."[11]

The most thoroughgoing exposition of the New Morality is presented by Prof. Joseph Fletcher in his book *Situation Ethics: The New Morality*.[12] He reasons that there are basically three approaches to making moral decisions: (1) legalism, (2) antinomianism, and (3) situationism. Rules and regulations reign in legalism. They are not merely guidelines or maxims; they are directives to be followed. Antinomianism (which literally means "against law") goes to the opposite extreme. Every situation is considered unique and therefore there can be no rules, maxims, or principles. "One must rely upon the situation of itself, *there and then,* to provide its ethical solution."[13] Situationism falls between legalism and antinomianism. The situationist has respectful awareness of the ethical maxims of his community and its heritage, but he is prepared "to compromise them or set them aside in the situation if love seems better served by doing so."[14] Love is the only norm, principle, or law of situation ethics. All other things are contingent, only valid if they serve love in the particular decision-making situation.

Thus for the situationist there can be conflicts of goals or ends of the various groups in a situation, but not of values. For him there is only one value: Christian love. It is up to the decision maker to determine which decision best serves the needs of love.

Models for Making Socially Responsible Decisions

There are four models for making socially responsible decisions which can be derived from the foregoing discussion of decision making under conditions of value conflict:

1   The equilibrium model
2   The incremental model
3   The computer model
4   The situational model

The strategic problem in making socially responsible decisions is how to choose among competing values. One way for the manager to deal with this problem is to attempt to maintain an equilibrium relationship among the welfare of the various groups affected by his decisions. This is the essence of the equilibrium model. Rather than set himself up as an expert on what is good for society, the manager views himself as an impartial umpire. His objective is to make decisions whose consequences are tolerable to each of the parties concerned. This approach minimizes the importance of the manager's subjective evaluation of the values involved in a decision-making situation and obviates the necessity for him to rank them. It is a political rather than a moral approach to decision making. The manager assesses the impact of the decision on various groups and selects the alternative which on balance will be received with the least dissent. The criterion of a good decision is lack of overt conflict.

The advantage of such an approach is that the manager does not over-estimate his capacity to deal with complex problems of value interpretation and evaluation. He assumes that the groups affected by his decision know more about its impact on their welfare than he does and will make their reactions known to him through regular channels. Management decisions at any moment of time bring into equilibrium relationship the interests of the groups involved. Any shift in power or other condition affecting the welfare of the groups will lead to a different emphasis in decision making. This is a practical approach. The manager may not know what is "right" in a given decision-making situation, but he is enough of a politician to be able to determine which alternative is likely to be most acceptable.

There are four criticisms to the equilibrium model. First, it implies there is no such thing as "the public interest" and that business decisions are merely an amalgam which reflects the relative power positions of contending interests. This is a proposition which many political scientists would not accept. Second, there is no assurance an equilibrium achieved in this way maximizes the total welfare of all groups affected by the decision. There may be undue consideration given to the most articulate groups. Third, managers are pictured as being much weaker and accommodating than they actually are. They are subject to the influence of external pressures, to be sure, but they have enough autonomy to resist them with vigor when deemed necessary. Fourth, the equilibrium approach to decision making has no ethical content. Management bases its decisions not on moral principle but on expediency, and expediency can never be offered as a *moral* reason for a particular action or decision. All that the plea of expediency does is to describe why something was done, not what *ought* to have been done.

Closely related to the equilibrium model is the incremental model. The manager approaches his task of making socially responsible decisions humbly, but he does attempt to move the world in some small measure in the direction of an optimal state. He does not explicitly sort out values involved in the decision and rank them, because this would confuse rather than clarify matters. Relying on intuition, he assesses the current situation and attempts to make a decision which improves things slightly. This is a conservative approach. Political factors are taken into account, but the manager is also actively involved in the moral aspects of the situation. By avoiding extremes he is not likely to commit a serious moral error, except perhaps by omission.

An example of this approach might be the impact of the civil rights movement on hiring and personnel practices. The manager might be besieged by various groups concerned with civil rights to take steps regarding the hiring of Negroes. Some groups would want more Negroes hired, readier access to management positions for Negroes, and so on, while others might want the company to maintain the status quo or even become more discriminatory in personnel practices. The manager who makes a decision on this matter according to the incremental model might decide to throw out any existing discriminatory practices and make hiring and advancement strictly a matter of ability.

The rational-deductive approach appears to have ready application to business decision making. Suppose that decisions are made in a company on the basis of the following three values and general principles derived from them: (1) profit (this company will attempt to earn the highest possible profit consistent with prudent management of its assets); (2) individualism (the affairs of this company will be conducted in ways consistent with the inherent dignity of the individual); and (3) progress (wherever possible new and better techniques of production and distribution will be developed and utilized). Further suppose that a decision must be made about whether or not to automate part of the production process. Let us assume that such a step would favor the profit and progress values but go against the value of individualism. To make a decision in such a situation, it is necessary to develop intermediate principles which govern the application of the general principles in specific instances. For example, an intermediate principle derived from the value of individualism might be, "Whenever an innovation eliminates the job of an employee, he will be given the opportunity to shift to another position in the company at no loss in pay or seniority." Such an intermediate principle would make it possible to make the decision to automate, but to carry out the process in a way which is in harmony with the set of ultimate values.

The rational-deductive approach is logically impeccable, but there are practical problems in applying it. The number of values, general principles, and intermediate principles involved in any decision-making situation is potentially vast because of the complexity of the social environment of business and the large number of variables in business decisions. The unaided human brain is inadequate to the task of organizing and operating such a system, but the electronic computer can do the job. Therefore, the computer model is restricted to those companies with computer facilities and the staff needed to gather the facts required by the intermediate principles. Even where such facilities are available, decisions deduced by computer should be viewed by top management as hypotheses to be tested against the subjective wisdom and judgment it has developed over the years through practical experience.

The decision-making method of situation ethics can be applied directly to the business world. The New Morality is more concerned with methodology than content. Its basic proposition is that in decision-making situations involving value conflict, there is no way of setting up a moral system which provides a solution. It views the equilibrium model as antinominal (i.e., *ad hoc,* based on no general moral principle) and the computer model as legalistic. The situational model hinges on the acceptance of social responsibility in a way similar to the acceptance of Christian love in the New Morality. It cannot be spelled out to fit possible future decision-making situations. Each case must be analyzed separately. It is up to the manager to determine what the socially responsible decision is in the decision-making situation he faces.

This model most heavily emphasizes individual responsibility and freedom. The manager who uses it is on his own. He must face up squarely to the moral aspects of the situation. He must grapple with the problem of conflicting values and be prepared to defend his judgment against criticisms from the parties affected. This approach requires courage, insight, and a speculative turn of mind. It is likely to work well only for managers who are well on the way to being moral philosophers; but when the prerequisites are met, the results can be spectacularly successful. Of the four models discussed, it best fits the American manager's self-image of a tough-minded individual who demands freedom and is willing and able to be responsible in its exercise.

Effective Role Playing by Socially Responsible Managers

Robert Austin suggested that the way to resolve the confusion and controversy about business ethics is to promulgate a code of conduct for executives or a creed for corporations. The basis of a code for the professional manager should be that he (1) places the interest of the corporation above his own; (2) places his duty to society above his duty to his corporation; (3) has a duty to reveal the facts in any situation of conflict of interests; and (4) realizes that when he adheres to this code the profit motive is the best business incentive.[15] Berle goes one step further with the idea that someday there will be a manual to which managers may refer when making decisions involving ethical judgment. A great many corporations have set down explicit company creeds in recent years. Their purpose is to formalize and clarify the firm's basic philosophy and objectives; to guide basic operating procedures; and to improve corporate relations with employees, stockholders, customers, and the public.[16]

None of these techniques is likely to clarify the ethical dimension of business with which the business statesmen must wrestle. Codes of conduct and corporate creeds may be of some use (certainly they do no harm) in capturing dramatically the essence of the spirit of an enterprise and its management. If they attempt to give a rule for every contingency, however, they become encyclopedic and hopelessly unwieldy. It may take nothing short of a book to communicate the philosophy of top management, and few businessmen are prepared to write such a book. A condensed version is likely to be merely a set of very broad statements with which nobody disagrees, but which are so general as to have no unique or easily perceived application in specific situations. On the other hand, Berle's notion of a manual for business statesmen seems impractical. Each decision calling for ethical judgment is unique and defies neat categorization as a precedent.

Much of the confusion and controversy about business ethics is due to the belief that here is one particular set of expectations that govern management behavior; and that once these are learned, it is simply a matter of doing what is expected of one. Such a static interpretation is at odds with the dynamic nature of life and business in America. The socially responsible manager's role is inherently dynamic because it is geared to social change. As we have seen, in the broadest sense the role expectations of the socially responsible manager consist of a generalized readiness to carry out society's will in the economic sphere. Society is always moving in some direction, but at any one time it is difficult to interpret the social drift. Consequently, it is not easy for managers to know exactly what is expected of them or the corporation at any particular time. Thus business ethics is never in a state of being; it is always in a process of becoming. A manager should never reach the point where he is certain for all time to come of his ethical position. To do so would be as foolish as to be sure for all time to come of the state of technology.

To be effective, a socially responsible manager must be tuned in to broad social trends and comprehend their significance for the corporation. This involves scanning the corporate environment for potential threats and opportunities. It is not enough, however, for the manager to have an outward orientation. He must be able to evaluate the importance and significance of what he sees in terms of ideas that have meaning for him and values in which he believes. In short, he must be rational and to be rational he must have a management philosophy upon which he can depend. Philosophy does three things: (1) It defines what is true; (2) it determines which questions are important to ask and rules others out; and (3) it prescribes a set of values useful in making decisions about right and wrong.

Carl Stover has pointed out that there have been three major trends in management philosophy in recent decades:[17]

1 *From management folklore to management science:* management has become an important object of scientific inquiry in its own right.
2 *From morality to morale:* the trend toward human relations in business.
3 *From mechanistic to dynamic approaches:* greater awareness of the changes in organizations, their participants, and the environment.

The management philosophies of socially responsible managers sensitive to trends in society and the business community have evolved in accordance with these trends.

Alfred North Whitehead considered foresight the key quality of mind of executives who think greatly of their functions. In an address at the Harvard Business School in 1930, he contrasted understanding and routine in business. He characterized routine as "the good of every social system . . . the seventh heaven of business, the essential component in the success of every factory."[18] But as much as the manager might like to run his business according to rationally conceived routines, he cannot.

"The point is that in the past the time span of important change was considerably longer than that of a single human life. Thus mankind was trained to adapt itself to fixed conditions. But today this time span is considerably shorter than that of human life, and accordingly our training must prepare individuals to face a novelty of conditions. But there can be no preparation for the unknown."[19] Whitehead concluded that business of the future must be controlled by a different type of leader, what we are referring to as the socially responsible manager. The question is, Where do these people come from and where do they get training in "foresight"? Whitehead saw the universities as the training ground for managers who have "the habit of transforming observation of qualitative changes into quantitative estimates," and "an unspecialized aptitude for eliciting generalizations from particulars and for seeing the divergent illustration of generalities in diverse circumstances."[20] This habit of general thought he considered the gift of philosophy.

Are our business schools turning out young men who aspire to be philosopher-executives? Drucker, writing twenty years after Whitehead, thought not. He said, "The business schools have 'arrived' without quite knowing what their job is, or how to accomplish it."[21] Drucker believes that professional business education should be built around three centers: (1) economic performance and profitability (i.e., how to be a good businessman); (2) internal administration—the problem of human organization; (3) the relationship of business enterprise and of management to society and economics. The basic question facing the business schools, according to Drucker, is not what kind of students it should teach but what is the function of business in the American economy? "The fervent arguments today take the form of a discussion of the curriculum or of the courses that should be offered. But at the bottom it is a discussion of the purpose and the function of the businessman in American society."[22]

Contrary to what is generally assumed, managers are not the only ones who make management decisions. Society has rejected the idea that management has an unequivocal right to use corporate resources in any way it sees fit. Managers are given power with strings attached. If they are to retain power, they must accept the fact that there are groups in society whose interests must be served. As Fred Munson put it, they must realize there are partners in management to whom managers must relate in a responsible way. "This willingness to accept a broader responsibility is a more sophisticated way to retain power, and a much more effective one than demanding power as a right."[23]

On the other hand, there are limits to social responsibility. There is the danger that managers who are socially oriented may see themselves as the shapers of the social destiny. Munson concludes, "Whether by ignoring other interest groups or trying to accept them as additional masters, the American way of life is unfriendly to the idea of managers being sole power centers for decisions made within the firm."[24] This suggests another factor in effective role playing by the socially responsible manager: He must clearly recognize the nature of the rights and obligations that characterize his interactions with other actors in the social system of the economy.

The key question concerning expectations of the socially responsible manager's role is, "Can he combine a self-interest orientation with a collectivity orientation?" In other words, can a socially responsible manager reasonably be expected to balance the interests of his enterprise against those of the economy and society? Theoretically there is no reason why this cannot be so. This relation between individual and collective interests exists in other roles—for example that of the United States senator. Voters recognize that senators are constantly forced by circumstances to balance the interests of their states with those of the nation. But there still is a suspicion that managers when faced with a choice between profit and the national interest will always choose the former. To a large extent, managers have themselves to blame for this attitude. They cannot expect the public to think of them more favorably than they think of themselves. Management needs a new self-image. Perhaps this is the motivation behind the great tide of speeches, articles, and books by businessmen about social responsibility.

The Dynamics of Social Responsibility

There is no such thing as "the blind play of economic forces." Economic activity is the result of decisions made by individuals, and individual behavior is controlled by cultural norms. Economizing is too important to the preservation of society and conflict over scarce economic values occurs too frequently to allow economic activity to go its own way without social regulation. The economic system is a web of expectations about how people behave or ought to behave. As Durkheim showed, there is a noncontractual element in contract. Fulfillment of contractual obligations must be explained in terms of the dependability of economic promises as well as the immediate interests of the contracting parties. Not even economic rationality can be taken for granted as a fixed characteristic because of its dependence upon complex conditions underlying the total social and cultural structure.

The goals the businessman strives for and the means he uses to attain them are culturally determined. The profit ethic can exist only because it is compatible with the underlying value orientation of society. But to say that society allows a self-seeking orientation to individual economic behavior is not to suggest that there is a complete absence of regulatory controls. The businessman may be free to maximize profit within his decision-making field of action, but this field of action has a boundary of cultural constraints. Only certain kinds of profit-making decisions are considered legitimate at any period of time. Decisions falling beyond the boundary are considered socially irresponsible, if not illegal.

In any period the norms governing economic activity are well established and relatively static, but over time changes occur in them. An analogy can be drawn between the economic short and long run and the cultural short and long run. In the economic short run, the businessman's plant is fixed; but in the economic long run, it can be varied. In the cultural short run, the norms governing economic activity are fixed; but in the cultural long run, they vary. Thus a decision which once was made on the basis of the profit ethic and was perfectly acceptable in time may be considered socially irresponsible because of changes in cultural norms.

The dynamic relationship between profit maximizing and socially responsible decisions is shown in the accompanying diagram. The circle in time period I represents the cultural constraints on profit-maximizing behavior. Profit-maximizing decisions may be made within the boundary or outside of it. Any decision made within the boundary is socially responsible in terms of the norms for behavior prevailing at the time. A decision made on the basis of the profit ethic which falls outside the profit-maximizing boundary is considered improper or socially irresponsible. Decision X falls within the boundary and therefore is socially responsible. At a later date, in time period II, the profit-maximizing boundary has shrunk and the range of socially irresponsible behavior has expanded. The same decision X now falls outside of the profit-maximizing boundary and is socially irresponsible.

Time period I

Time period II

Why has the profit-maximizing boundary shrunk? It seems likely that in the early stages of capitalistic development the need for profit is greater than at a more advanced stage. Therefore, entrepreneurs will be allowed greater freedom by society to pursue profit than will managers at a later and higher stage of capitalism. An example is the use of child labor in industry. In the Industrial Revolution, children labored long hours in dangerous and wretched working conditions. Factory owners felt few moral qualms about this practice. Society accepted it as necessary and therefore socially responsible. This no longer is the case. It is socially irresponsible to hire children for dangerous and unhealthy work, and factory owners do not do so. This stricture would exist even if there were no child labor laws because the normative system is so ingrained in employers that few of them would go against the social consensus.

Under some circumstances the profit-maximizing boundary may expand rather than contract, and a wider range of profit-maximizing behavior will be allowed. A case in point is the Russian textile industry where the profit ethic is being used to make decisions on an experimental basis to see if the performance of the industry can be improved. The experience in the United States, however, supports the idea of a shrinking profit-maximizing boundary.

This analysis offers a clue as to why managers resist the notion of social responsibility. They think of themselves as hard-driving profit maximizers who have little patience for the broader issues of society and leave these matters to ministers, professors, and social workers. In a way they are right—they are concerned in the conscious part of their minds with

Making socially responsible decisions

173

profit making. But in a fundamental sense they are wrong. They fail to take into account the constraints on profit making which have just as much effect on their decisions as the desire to earn profit. They have an essentially static view of their own behavior and therefore take a good deal for granted without realizing it. But the cultural constraints change over time. It is not at all uncommon for a man of many years' business experience to suddenly realize the great gulf between the kinds of decisions he makes today compared with thirty or forty years ago. He would not dream of doing today what he did then. But he is still a profit maximizer in his own mind. What has happened in the interim, of course, is that society has changed the rules of the game and he has learned the new rules almost without knowing it. He has become socially responsible in spite of himself!

Social Responsibility as a Point of View

The analysis of this chapter suggests that social responsibility is more a point of view, a way of looking at things, than an explicit ethic. There is no simple decision-making rule that can be universally applied in situations involving morality and ethics. This, of course, explains the great attraction of the profit ethic. The rule is completely unambiguous—always select the decision which maximizes profit. But what does it mean to say, "Be socially responsible—always select the decision which maximizes social utility"? There are a host of philosophical questions that lurk behind such an injunction, and the socially responsible manager cannot avoid them. The quest for a single, simple, and universal action rule is futile. The only things that a socially responsible manager can do are (1) understand the nature of his status and role; (2) develop a management philosophy that helps keep his role expectations in focus; (3) reach an understanding of his own values; (4) develop a technique for reaching a decision in situations of value conflict; (5) remain alert to social trends that affect the corporation and management; and (6) take his courage in his hands and deal with each policy-making and decision-making situation as it arises with an awareness that there are no final answers and that errors in judgment are bound to occur but that such errors will be minimized if the moral and ethical dimension of policies and decisions is faced head on.

NOTES

1   Talcott Parsons, *Structure and Process in Modern Society* (New York: The Free Press of Glencoe, 1960), chaps. 1 and 2.

2   Manley Howe Jones, *Executive Decision Making* (Homewood, Ill.: Richard Richard D. Irwin, Inc., 1962), p. 339.

3   Philip Selznick, *Leadership in Administration* (New York: Harper & Row, Publishers, Incorporated, 1957), p. 5.

4   *Ibid.,* p. 17.

5   *Ibid.,* p. 28.

6   Herbert A. Simon, *Administrative Behavior* (New York: The Macmillan Company, 1957), pp. 45–46.

7   Wayne A. R. Leys, "Ethics and Administrative Discretion," *Administrative Review* (Winter, 1943), p. 17.

8   Kenneth J. Arrow, *Social Choice and Individual Values* (New York: John Wiley & Sons, Inc., 1951), p. 22.

9   David Braybrooke and Charles E. Lindblom, *A Strategy of Decision* (New York: The Free Press of Glencoe, 1963), pp. 84–85.

10 Karl Popper, *The Open Society and Its Enemies,* vol. 1 (London: Routledge & Kegan Paul, Ltd., 1945), pp. 139–144.

11 Paul Tillich, *Systematic Theology,* vol. 1 (Chicago: The University of Chicago Press, 1951), p. 152.

12 Joseph Fletcher, *Situation Ethics: The New Morality* (Philadelphia: The Westminster Press, 1966).

13 *Ibid.,* p. 22.

14 *Ibid.,* p. 26.

15 Robert W. Austin, "Code of Conduct for Executives," *Harvard Business Review,* vol. 39, no. 5 (September–October, 1961), p. 60.

16 Stewart Thompson, *Management Creeds and Philosophies* (New York: American Management Association, 1958), p. 37.

17 Carl F. Stover, "Changing Patterns in the Philosophy of Management," *Public Administration Review,* vol. 18, no. 1 (Winter, 1958), pp. 23–27. (Italics supplied.)

18 Alfred North Whitehead, "On Foresight," introduction to Wallace Brett Donham, *Business Adrift* (New York: McGraw-Hill Book Company, 1931); reprinted in Edward C. Bursk et al. (eds.), *The World of Business,* vol. IV (New York: Simon & Schuster, Inc., 1962), p. 2047.

19 *Ibid.,* p. 2050.

20 *Ibid.,* p. 2054.
21 Peter F. Drucker, "The Graduate Business School," *Fortune,* vol. 42, part 1 (August, 1950), p. 92.
22 *Ibid.,* p. 114.
23 Fred C. Munson, "Partners in Management," *Michigan Business Review,* vol. 17, no. 5 (November, 1965), p. 2.
24 *Ibid.,* p. 3.

Index